A Brief History
of the
Church of God Reformation Movement

By John W. V. Smith

warnerpress

ANDERSON, INDIANA

Warner Press, Inc
Warner Press and "Warner Press" logo are trademarks of Warner Press, Inc

A Brief History of the Church of God Reformation Movement
Written by John W.V. Smith

First edition 1956
Second edition 1976
Third edition 2006

Requests for information should be sent to:
Warner Press, Inc.
2902 Enterprise Drive
Anderson, IN 46013
www.warnerpress.org

Editors: Joseph D. Allison and Stephen R. Lewis
Cover: Mary Jaracz
Appendix by Stephen R. Lewis
Index by Joseph D. Allison and Stephen R. Lewis

ISBN: 978-1-59317-140-7

warner press

TABLE OF CONTENTS

INTRODUCTION

Scores of religious bodies in the United States employ a version of the New Testament phrase "Church of God" as their official name. A congregation in Indianapolis even proclaims itself "The Original Church of God." Over the last 125 years, one fellowship came to call itself the Church of God reformation movement. In histories and directories of American religion it is known as the Church of God (Anderson, Indiana). By either name it is the tradition that John W. V. Smith studied from his graduate student days at the University of Southern California until his sudden and premature death more than twenty years ago. Over the course of his long tenure at Anderson University's School of Theology, Professor Smith wrote several important historical narratives and analyses of the Church of God.

One of his earliest books, published in 1956, was a slender volume titled *Truth Marches On*. Twenty years later, Professor Smith revised and enlarged that book and it was printed as the present volume. Now Church of God Ministries is once again making this helpful study available.

Truth Marches On appeared at a moment when Church of God leaders possessed unbridled optimism about the movement and its future. During the decade of the 1950s, many groups in America continued to prosper in a religious revival that had begun shortly after the end of World War II. President Dwight Eisenhower openly endorsed deeply felt religious faith as a cornerstone of national life. Public service advertisements on television encouraged Americans to attend the church or synagogue of their choice, and the motto "In God We Trust" made its first appearance on United States currency. This rising tide of religious interest raised all boats, including the Church of God. From 1950 to 1960, Church of God membership[1] grew by 32 percent to 128,000 souls. Between 1940 and 1970, membership more than doubled, and the aggregate value of church property, excluding college campuses and church offices, reached $125 million. In 1956 the church had recently concluded a successful "Mid-Century Evangelistic Campaign" and everywhere signs pointed to a bright and hopeful future.

By the time Warner Press released Professor Smith's revised and enlarged volume as *A Brief History of the Church of God Reformation Movement* in 1976, both the church and American society had endured much that could not have been imagined twenty years earlier. Assassinations had struck down a president, his brother, and a civil rights leader; television brought these violent and tragic scenes directly into American living rooms. The civil rights movement had introduced words like *segregation* and *integration* into public consciousness. The United States had also withdrawn its military and naval forces from a place called Viet Nam after a long, unsuccessful, and unpopular war. Richard Nixon's administration was brought down by the Watergate scandal, but three astounding performances by a horse named Secretariat finally gave the American public a hero that everybody could cheer. The Church of God also experienced something of the ferment of those years. Students at its colleges had marched for civil rights and later joined antiwar protests. In 1970, the Caucus of

---

[1]Church of God congregations have no official membership records as a matter of theological convinction; for many years, each pastor reported a congregation's active constituency in the annual *Yearbook* as "membership." The *Yearbook* now reports average attendance figures instead.

Black Churchmen in the Church of God met in Cleveland, Ohio to publicize the burden and concerns of African-Americans in the church. The dramatic growth in membership began leveling off and some church leaders called for new forms of evangelism.

Thirty years have passed since the first release of Professor Smith's revised history. As in the years between 1956 and 1976, much in the Church of God has changed during these three decades. The national organization of agencies and commissions has undergone substantial restructuring. The church's venerable paper, *Vital Christianity*, ceased publication in 1996 after a run of more than a century. The rate of membership growth increased, but the number of Church of God adherents outside North America has grown more rapidly; today the church's non-North American constituency outnumbers North Americans by more than two to one. Worship styles have changed dramatically, and new music and choruses are in many quarters replacing the hymns and gospel songs of an earlier day. Finally, although the Counterculture of the '70s was not successful at recruiting many young people into Eastern religions, its influence has pervaded much of American Christianity and the Church of God in the laidback, informal style that has become a commonplace of worship and other public meetings.

Professor Smith enlarged *Truth Marches On* in order to place greater emphasis on the church. He rightly understood that a particular vision of the church was central to both the doctrinal tradition of the Church of God and to its very beginning and development. In the theological history of the Church of God, the doctrine of the church often lay just beneath the surface of debates on holiness or the kingdom of God or eschatology; the rhetoric may have concerned one of these topics, but the real issue was the church. Smith believed that the doctrinal theme and development of the church must play a prominent role in a historical narrative of the Church of God.

In the face of dramatic change over the thirty years since its first release, *A Brief History of the Church of God Reformation Movement* remains a valuable resource for the church. Then or now, few if any persons can match Professor Smith's comprehensive knowledge of the Church of God and his ability to synthesize that information in a readable narrative. In 1980, he brought out his magnum opus, *The Quest for Holiness and Unity*, still the finest comprehensive history of the Church of God. But the smaller *Brief History* remains an ideal introduction to the movement and thus is ideally suited for newcomers or as the basis for a quarterly study of the Church of God. It is through such studies that we encounter the narrative of a people animated by a strong sense of divine vocation. They believed that God had called them to a double-edged witness. One side of that witness was directed to a world in need of a Savior, while the other witnessed to a deeply divided Christendom. Professor Smith's *Brief History* faithfully recounts the developments of that two-sided mission and the movement's strong belief that disunity among Christians only served to frustrate their evangelistic labor. When we read and ponder such narratives we come to a clearer sense of identity, and out of this clearer sense we understand better the mission to which the church is called today. Furthermore, at a moment in American church life when individualistic conceptions of Christianity abound, Smith's reminder that a vision of the church is at the heart of the Church of God movement reminds us that to be saved in Christ is also to be admitted to the fellowship of his Body, the church.

Merle D. Strege
Historian of the Church of God

FOREWORD

This book is a considerably revised and expanded version of an earlier publication, *Truth Marches On*. It is retitled for two specific reasons: (1) to indicate that the rather extensive rewriting and updating of the material make this more than simply a new edition of the previous work, and (2) to give more definite emphasis to the centrality of the doctrine of the church in the emergence and development of this religious reform movement, known generally as the Church of God (Anderson, Indiana).

A study of the history of this nineteenth-century movement reveals that both its original and continuing reason for being lies in a burning concern to lift up and live out certain biblical insights regarding the nature of God's church which are particularly appropriate for our time. The new title suggests the lofty and aspirational character of these particular insights. The early leaders of the movement not only decried the "Babel confusion" of a divided and imperfect church but also envisioned a full restoration of God's one church with biblical truth as its only creed and holiness as its most evident characteristic. They conceived their mission to be both the proclamation of this vision and the identification of a visible fellowship open to every person who could testify to being a redeemed child of God.

To these reformers this "light" on the church was more than the rediscovery of a historic doctrine and much more than the projection of a utopian dream. They understood the basic problem of a divided church and they were convinced they knew the solution to that problem. Excitedly they proclaimed their vision of a united and holy Church of God. By sermon and song and printed word these "flying messengers" announced that the "church triumphant" need not wait for a new age to be revealed, but was becoming a present reality. Lustily they sang,

"There's a mighty reformation sweeping o'er the land, God is gathering his people by his mighty hand," and "From all the divisions in which they were scattered, Thy children are gathering home." Another lyric declared:

The day of sects and creeds for us
forevermore is past,
Our brotherhood are all the saints
upon the world so vast;
We reach our hands in fellowship
to every blood-washed one,
While love entwines about each heart
in which God's will is done.

Beyond these jubilee affirmations there was clear and solid teaching about how this was to be accomplished. Redemption in Christ, acceptance of all biblical truth, and direction of both personal and corporate life by the Holy Spirit were basic. Even these theological concepts were lyricized as they sang, "I'm Redeemed," "Back to the Blessed Old Bible," and "The Bond of Perfectness." They "saw" the church of God, but they knew it was not theirs to construct or organize. A united church was not something to be fashioned by any person. As Daniel S. Warner put it: "O brethren how this perfect love unites us all in Jesus! One heart, and soul, and mind we prove the union heaven gave us."

One other aspect of the vision of these reformers needs to be noted: they saw a unified church as both a present visible reality and also as in process of becoming. They did not hesitate to refer to their small fellowship as the Church of God, but they knew this was not the whole church. In all their affirmations there is evident anticipation of a growing unity among all God's people. The realized fellowship was precious, but it was only the vanguard of what God intended it should be. The reformation is "sweeping o'er" the land; the children are "gathering" home; the Shepherd "has begun" to gather his long divided flock; division walls are "falling." Within this frame of reference the movement finds its impetus both in being able to say, "We *are* the church of God," and also, "We are not the whole church of God; we are God's agents for leading all true believers *toward* the realization of his will for his church—that they all may be one.

The purpose of this book, then, is to highlight our rich heritage from the people who put these insights together and published them with such vigor and dedication that a worldwide movement emerged within a few short years and which after almost a century, continues its witness in pointing the Christian world toward the church of God.

In presenting this book for general reading a few words ought to be said concerning the general nature of the work and some of its intended uses. To begin with, it will be noted that the book is brief. It does not presume to be a comprehensive history of the Church of God reformation movement. Many important leaders and numerous significant developments have not been included, both because of lack of space and because this particular book is designed only to lift up some of the main aspects of the movement's development for review and analysis. In the strictest sense of the word this is a historical study rather than a history. It is as much an attempt to interpret this reformation movement as it is to set down events.

In short, it is intended that this book will be used as the basis for both individual and group study. To assist in such study several points for discussion are listed at the end of each chapter. It will also be noted that the material is divided into twelve chapters, thus making it convenient to fit it into a one-quarter study for a Sunday school class. (The thirteenth Sunday could be used in developing the history and purposes of the local congregation.) The book may also be used as a text for study and quest groups, for a series of prayer meetings, and for pastor's classes with youth and adults. It may also serve as a supplemental resource in certain college and seminary classes.

In compiling this study, the author has sought to make it as authentic as possible by checking sources carefully and seeking verification at every point. Even so, the scantiness of records, the absence of original documents, and the limitations of memory make the story incomplete and difficult to reconstruct in many places. In addition to whatever other values this study may have it is hoped that it will also stimulate interest in the recovery of many records and other items of value in accurately understanding the heritage from the pioneers in this reformation movement.

—John W. V. Smith

Anderson, Indiana

CHAPTER I

THE BEGINNING OF A REFORMATION

In the almost two thousand years of its history the Christian church has experienced many reformations. Whenever truth has become enshrouded in error, whenever form has obscured spirit, and whenever essentials have been dropped by the way, there has always been a God-inspired person or movement seeking to restore the church to its true character as the body of Christ and the people of God.

Some of these reformations have been sudden, but others have developed over a period of time. Some have been drastic, revamping the whole existing structure, but many have involved only portions of the church's total activity. By their very nature some reforms have had universal implications, while others have come to focus on conditions purely local or regional. In general, it may be said that all of these reformations have aimed at one of more of four general objectives: (1) combating error which had crept into either doctrine or practice, (2) removing abuses, (3) changing outmoded procedures, or (4) reemphasizing some neglected aspect of the faith. Practically all reformers have looked upon their work as a restoration of the ideals of the early Christian church.

Religious Revolutions

The most widely known of all these reformations, of course, is the wave of reforming activity which swept across Europe in the sixteenth century. Under the leadership of such spiritual stalwarts as Martin Luther, Ulrich Zwingli, and John Calvin the whole pattern of medieval Christianity was drastically changed. With good reason some historians refer to this series of reforms as a religious revolution. The total impact of this revolution can never be determined, perhaps, but it can be partially realized by noting that out of the sixteenth century a new type of Christianity emerged—a type commonly designated as Protestantism.

The drastic and far-reaching sixteenth-century Reformation was not a reformation to end all reformations. Actually, the basic teachings of these reformers made it much easier for reforms to take place, so reformations have been more numerous since that time than they were before. In the seventeenth century, for example, a humble shoemaker's apprentice in England by the name of George Fox earnestly sought to find the reason for the barrenness of the Christianity in his own country. He experienced enlightenment regarding his own spiritual condition and began to speak out boldly against the shallowness and insincerity of the church people of his day. Thus began a reformation movement by the people called Quakers. They called for a renewal of genuine inward religion on the part of all believers.

In the eighteenth century two major reformation movements arose, both of which were aiming at the same purpose. In Germany, under the leadership of two university professors, Philipp Spener and August Hermann Francke, a movement known as Pietism came into existence. Pietistic views were to exert a great influence on the kind of Christianity which later developed in both England and America. In England, two Oxford students, John and Charles Wesley, were responsible for starting a "holy club" which evolved into a reform movement known as Methodism. Both the Pietists and the Methodists sought to restore deep personal piety and righteous living.

A New Reformation

In the latter part of the nineteenth century another major reformation began. This one is not nearly so well known as the others, but its impact is still in the process of being realized. In many respects this reformation resembles the earlier movements, for it also emphasized, almost without exception, the main points lifted up by previous reformers. There was strong preaching, for example, about the necessity of a genuine experience of justification by faith in Jesus Christ, sanctification by the Holy Spirit, and holiness in everyday living. Beyond these individual doctrines, however, there was a major emphasis on what all of these implied regarding the nature and unity of the church. Thus, this new movement sought to bring all truth and all Christians together into a unity of faith and fellowship which would enable the church to measure up to God's intention for it. From the standpoint of comprehensiveness no other reformation had ever approached the breadth of vision and the ambitious hope of this one. It was the intention of these reformers to restore the true church by bringing all faithful Christians into a visible, unified fellowship which would transcend all divisions and sects.

The early leaders of this movement were so caught up in a sense of significance for their message that they took great pains to keep from calling attention to themselves as persons. They regarded the developing response to their activity as a work of God and not the product of their own leadership. They took advantage of every opportunity to tell their story, but they neglected in most cases to keep a record of who did what and where and when events took place. Thus, it is very difficult to designate either an exact time or place for the beginning of this religious movement.

It is perhaps sufficient to say the Church of God reformation began in midwestern United States of America. The first apparent manifestations were in the states of Ohio, Indiana, and Michigan. It is customary to speak of 1880 as the year in which the movement started. From available information it would be much easier to designate 1877 or 1878 as crucial turning points in the lives of the early leaders. The first overt attempt to launch a movement, though, did not come until late in 1881. If we think in terms of a truly distinct movement we would have to say, then, that this was the time of beginning. It happened something like this.

How It Began

On a day in early October, 1881, a group of people from various localities in northern Indiana met in a little white church on the western edge of the small village of Beaver Dam. They were gathered for the official annual eldership meeting of the religious body to which they belonged, a small denomination known as the Northern Indiana Eldership of the Church of God. This group was only five years old. They had severed themselves from the parent group, the General Eldership of the Churches of God in North America (more commonly known as the Winebrennerian Church of God), because they thought the General Eldership was not upholding the proper standard in refusing to condemn membership in secret societies. A number of the congregations in northern Indiana had joined in the separation.

The new group had made reasonable progress during its short history, and the fresh fires of enthusiasm were still burning brightly. With gratitude they heard reports of progress from the various congregations. The chairman then asked for reports concerning some of the general phases of their work. Among those who were called upon to speak was the editor of the biweekly paper called the *Gospel Trumpet,* which the group considered its official publication even though all the equipment was owned by the editor, and he was given a free hand in regard to the management. D. S. Warner walked to the front of the church.

The Editor Speaks

When the thirty-nine-year-old Warner began to speak it was immediately apparent that his was not going to be just an ordinary report. As far as we know he said nothing about the number of subscriptions or the income and expenses in publishing the paper. Very obviously he had something urgent on his mind, so he quickly came to the point. One can imagine that his report went something like this. (Since there is no verbatim record of this meeting the quoted words are not, of course, an exact rendition of Warner's report. Based on available evidence, however, this reconstructed account attempts to be faithful to the actual event.):

"Brethren, as you know, it was just three years ago this week that I attended my first meeting of this Eldership. At that time you voted me into your fellowship and elected me associate editor of the *Herald of Gospel Freedom*. Later, after Brother Lowman's retirement, I became editor. Last winter the *Herald* was merged with another holiness paper called the *Pilgrim*, which was published in Indianapolis by a Brother Haines. We decided to call the new paper resulting from this merger the *Gospel Trumpet*. The first issue came out of the office in Rome City, Indiana, on January 1 of this year, 1881. In February we moved to Indianapolis. Shortly after that Brother Haines withdrew from the partnership, and I was forced to pay him for his interest. He took the money and started a rival paper in the same city, but, thank the Lord, we are continuing with our work despite the difficulties."

"Responsibility Before God"

After this brief introduction Warner then launched into the matter which was on his heart.

"Those of you who have been reading the *Trumpet*, particularly during the last several months, know that I have been holding high the banner of holiness and have been bearing down heavily on the sinful sectarian divisions in the church. I am becoming more convinced that God is now calling us to take some drastic steps. I see no other way to fulfill God's purpose than to abandon these unholy divisions completely and take our stand wholly apart from sectism.

"At the time I joined with you brethren in the Northern Indiana Eldership I was convinced that this group was upholding the standard of holiness and was freer from man-made rules than any other group of which I knew. I still believe that. It seems to me, though, that the time has come when we are going to have to make our position in regard to these truths even plainer than we have in the past. We must refuse to participate in any kind of endeavor which sanctions the sectarian system. I am referring specifically to the National Holiness Association. That organization, worthy though it may be, has refused to admit members except they first be members of some sect. As long as we participate in this Association, then, we are forced to sanction this sect-endorsing policy and are put in the position of approving that which is sinful. Our responsibility before God is to keep ourselves completely clear of everything that is unholy. I, therefore, propose that we sever our relations with this Association and declare ourselves to be joined with Christ alone."

"Who Will Stand Up?"

As Warner stopped speaking and walked toward his seat a hush fell on the whole group. The chairman was somewhat at a loss but finally stated the proposal and asked for discussion. It soon became apparent that not many were ready to take the step which had been suggested, and so no action was taken. But Warner was not willing to let the matter rest there. He again rose to his feet and began to speak.

"My good friends, my decision on this matter has already been made. God made it plain to me last summer that 'there is one body and one Spirit' (Eph. 4:4), and that he is displeased when men try to divide the body of Christ. At the Holiness Association meeting in Terre Haute in June, I withdrew from that organization when they refused to change the sect-endorsing clause in their bylaws. If this Eldership also refuses to take a stand against sectism then I shall be forced to sever my connections with this fellowship also, even though it hurts me deeply to do so."

Warner paused and looked over the assembly. Then, calmly but firmly he continued. "I have made no attempt to influence any of you unduly, but I do not feel that I stand alone in my convictions. If there are others here who feel that we should have no part in the sect spirit, I would like to know about it.

Would any of you care to stand up now and by so doing declare that you are free from all sectarian division and stand only in the one fold of all the redeemed?"

The dramatic hush which followed this question was broken after a moment as a man and his wife looked at each other and then rose to their feet. Another man joined them, and then another couple stood up—five in all. They were Mr. and Mrs. William Ballenger, David Leininger, and Mr. and Mrs. Frank Krause, all from the vicinity of Beaver Dam.

Within a short time this handful of people had arranged to begin holding services in their homes and in schoolhouses. Later they erected a small brick church building just west of the village. This was the first congregation of the Church of God reformation movement.

Who Was This Man Warner?

The man who had taken the lead in this memorable incident was not a "crackpot" who had suddenly appeared on the scene. Daniel Sidney Warner had been a Christian minister for fourteen years. He had been ordained by the General Eldership of the Churches of God in North America (Winebrennerian) and had served as pastor of several congregations in Ohio. He had also spent over two years in home missionary work in Nebraska. He had been successful in all of these ventures.

Warner had not been brought up in a Chr stian home, and it was not until he was almost twenty-three years old that he began to think seriously about religion. One February night in 1865 he went to a public altar in a schoolhouse revival meeting and was converted. From that time to the end of his life he continued diligently in his search for spiritual truth. He never ceased to have an open mind about his beliefs and methods of work. The first two years after his conversion were spent in college and in teaching public school. In 1867 he entered the ministry.

In the early years of Warner's career as a preacher he was a strong opponent of the doctrine of holiness which was coming to be emphasized in many churches. In the later 1870s, however, he became convinced that the experience of entire sanctification was scriptural, so he began to preach it with vigor. Somewhat to his surprise other ministers in his denomination became quite critical of his new emphasis. This led to difficulty which brought about the revocation of his license in January of 1878. He then became affiliated with the Northern Indiana Eldership. After three years, as we have seen, he found that fellowship too narrow for his expanding concept of truth.

A Movement Is Born

At the time Warner severed his connections with all sectarian organizations he probably felt as though he was pretty much alone in taking such a stand. It was not long, however, until he discovered that many others had been thinking along such lines for as long as or longer than he had. Within two weeks after the Beaver Dam incident a group of about twenty people in Carson City, Michigan, under the leadership of J. C. and Allie R. Fisher, took similar action and withdrew from the Northern Michigan Eldership, a religious body similar to the one with which Warner had been associated. The Fishers had had some contact with Warner previous to this time and Warner was present when the Carson City separation took place. Thus these two new congregations, even though they were almost two hundred miles apart, were drawn into fellowship with each other and became centers from which the truth they embraced could spread. An annual camp meeting was established at each of these places.

Within the next few months the movement began to take shape. Leaders from other churches heard of the stand which these people had taken and added their witness to those already proclaiming the message. A. J. Kilpatrick, for instance, a United Brethren minister in Ohio, had already arrived at the same viewpoint as Warner before the two ever met and had also declared himself to be free from sectarian bondage. Jeremiah Cole, a Methodist from Missouri who had been very active in the holiness movement, identified himself with the new work very early. Some of the more prominent leaders who "took their stand" by the mid 1880s were A. B. Palmer, Sebastian Michels, A. J. Shelly, and Barney Warren from Michigan; "Mother" Sarah Smith. W. J. Henry, and William N. Smith from Ohio; Samuel L. Speck and F. N. Jacobson from Illinois; George Clayton and W. B. Grover from Pennsylvania; Henry Wickersham from Indiana; and W. W. Roberts from Iowa. These and many others showed themselves to be vigorous "flying messengers" who proclaimed far and wide the "truth about the church" which had excited their own understanding.

Not Men but a Message

None of these early leaders in the Church of God had any intention of launching a new religious organization. In fact, the existence of separated Christian denominations was the thing they most abhorred. Division was the basic evil from which they were trying to escape. They were simply a group of people with a message which they felt was so important that they could not keep from proclaiming it. They had seen the "light." They were possessors of the great realization that the will of God could never be fully accomplished until all true Christians were joined together in a common witness. So they took a full step forward, insisting that not only must the redeemed live righteous lives, they must also be in fellowship and harmony with each other. On the basis of these fundamental principles the Church of God reformation movement was launched into a world that desperately needed just such a vital and positive message.

Points for Discussion

1. What are the basic reasons why reformations have occurred in the Christian church?
2. What do all religious reformations have in common?
3. In what specific ways does the Church of God reformation resemble previous reformations? In what ways is it different?

4. What were the particular circumstances which produced the Church of God reformation?

5. In withdrawing from their various denominations and launching a new movement, how were Warner and the other leaders consistent with their message of Christian unity?

Chapter II

THE NATURE OF THIS REFORMATION

Before proceeding with the story of how the Church of God reformation developed it would be well to take a broad overview of the religious and secular conditions which created the climate of need for a reformation such as this. Only then can the essential nature of the movement and its relationship to the whole of Christianity be understood. Such an analysis is important, for subsequent developments are in great measure the product of the original dynamics which brought the movement into being, and the ideals which were articulated in the primitive period of the group's history are projected into its whole future. In order that the movement be seen in proper perspective, three general observations regarding the character of this new reformation are set forth as being particularly significant.

Related to Real Issues

The first observation about this movement is that from the very beginning it was closely related to the life of the people and the issues of the time. The foundations of this religious reformation were laid in the soil of rural America and fashioned of basic Christian principles as they applied to the life of the people who lived there. There was no new mysterious revelation to a prophet, no new philosophical system, not even a new scholarly interpretation of Christian theology. The chief religious concerns of the early leaders and those who joined with them were the close-to-life matters of midwestern America in the late nineteenth century. A look at these conditions is necessary if one is to have a proper understanding of the developments which took place.

The period following the American Civil War saw marked changes in religious attitudes and interests. Both the thinking and the practice of Christian churches were in a process of transition. In the older churches along the Atlantic seaboard a strong reaction against the revivalism of an earlier time had developed and was accompanied by more than a slight tendency toward a new liberalism in theology, with many basic beliefs being called into question. The low moral tone of society in general brought a wave of religious accommodation to worldly standards, and a spirit of secularism came to dominate many of the clergy and their congregations. Practically all churches were much less insistent than formerly on a definite religious experience as a qualification for membership, with the result that the line between the "saved" and the "unsaved" became less and less distinct. In general, the witness of the churches was not a vital one. People were more interested in discussing Darwin's *On the Origin of Species* than in obtaining salvation for their souls.

In the middle West these same tendencies were also in evidence, despite the postwar efforts of some of the churches to conduct revivals. In the main it may be said that the dying embers of evangelistic zeal were divided among the various denominations and were used to start new fires of loyalty to the separate groups. This resurgent sectarianism resulted in a sharper drawing of the lines which separated Christians from each other, and bitter rivalry arose among the several competing denominations. Schism broke the ranks of some of the larger communions and a number of new competitors entered the field through this splintering process. This was indeed the heyday of militant sectarianism.

The total impact of all this competitive activity did not bring any life to American Christianity, however. With certain notable exceptions it may be said that the churches of this period had a shortened view of their mission and a distorted sense of direction. The Great Commission was usually defined in terms of making additions to the membership rolls—often at the expense of other groups who were trying to do the same. Obviously this was a goal far short of the New Testament challenge to preach the gospel of love and repentance. In the main it may be said that the American Christianity of this time was generally shallow and was moving in the direction of disunity and competition rather than toward unity and cooperation.

One cooperative venture, however, transcended the barriers of denominationalism and sought to remedy some of the existing evils. This was the holiness movement. Although a loosely organized enterprise, its efforts never completely coordinated, the National Association for the Promotion of Holiness, first organized in Vineland, New Jersey, in July of 1867, was a concrete expression of a rather widespread desire to restore genuine Christian piety. Through sponsoring holiness camp meetings and encouraging the distribution of holiness literature, this organization sought to promote the preaching of experiential religion, particularly the doctrine of sanctification, among the various ministers who were receptive to this kind of emphasis. The leaders were very careful, however, to do no violence to the denominational system. In most instances membership in a denomination was necessary in order to be a member of the Association. Thus, the believers in holiness were given opportunity to stand against the wickedness and shallow religion of the day, but in so doing they were forced to defend the disunity of the church and the competitive character of its witness.

D. S. Warner and many of the other early leaders of the Church of God reformation were associated with the holiness movement. They were attracted by the positive emphasis on personal piety which they found among these brethren. They were free to appropriate the truths which had been lifted up by the holiness people, but they were not satisfied to let the unhealthy condition of the church itself go unchallenged. In a most straightforward manner they came to grips with this issue and pointed an accusing finger at the sinful divisions in the body of Christ. These bold men issued a call to sincere Christians everywhere to sever their relations with "sectism" and to stand in the truth of God alone. They had no finespun theological theories to promote, but they were greatly concerned about the tragically divided state of the church. They sought to restore its unity and holiness in the most direct way possible.

It thus becomes apparent that the Church of God reformation was born out of a deep sensitivity to the acute needs of Christianity as it existed at this particular time and place in history. The movement is to be understood and its genius is to be explained only as this life-situation context is recognized. Any later tendencies in the group to be aloof from the grass-roots problems of the Christian world or any inclinations to define its mission in purely theoretical terms are strictly departures from the original character of the movement. The early leaders were not ivory-tower dreamers. They were close to the needs of their world, and their strategy for meeting those needs was direct action.

In the Mainstream of Christianity

A second observation about the Church of God movement is that it is completely within the stream of historic Christianity. There is nothing about it which can be considered off-brand or heretical. Many recent analysts of the movement have noted that the early leaders did not introduce a single new doctrine. The major truths they emphasized and the basic theological insights they preached had been set forth previously in Christian history by some recognized leader. None of the great essentials of historic Christianity were dropped, and nothing of an extraneous nature was added. These leaders were neither rebels nor anarchists, yet the reforms they advocated were so sweeping that they were considered revolutionary even by other participants in the holiness movement.

How could a movement so thoroughly orthodox in doctrine be considered revolutionary? The answer is to be found first in the fact that this was a true reformation in that it sought to bring about fundamental changes in structures and practices, even to the point of destroying the whole entrenched denominational system. That is revolutionary. Furthermore, while it is true that these early leaders emphasized certain points more than they did others, it is also true that they were committed to the acceptance and preaching of *all truth* which could be authenticated by the Word of God. That is revolutionary. These reformers were not bound by any written creed, and they were careful to avoid composing one of their own. The horizon of truth was as broad as man's comprehension of the Bible and the revelation of the Spirit would allow. Such an attitude led toward a comprehensiveness in emphasis which had seldom been seen in Christianity since the first century. Some analysts of the movement have asserted that this inclusive combination of truths previously taught only in part by other groups in Christian history constitutes the unique contribution of the Church of God.

One other point needs to be made, however, in regard to the relationship of this movement to the rest of Christianity, particularly Protestantism. The reformers of the sixteenth century directed their efforts mainly toward the correction of certain abuses in both doctrine and practice which had developed in the Roman Catholic Church. Their thinking led to a reemphasis on at least three points of doctrine which had been neglected or distorted by the Roman church—justification by faith, the priesthood of all believers, and the sufficiency of the Bible as a basis for authority. In the seventeenth century George Fox placed special emphasis on the direct work of the Spirit of God in revealing truth to man. Over a century later the Wesleyan reform reissued the call to personal piety and came to focus primarily in an emphasis on the sanctifying work of the Holy Spirit. It is noteworthy that all these previous reforming movements were basically concerned with doctrines involving the individual and his personal relationship to God.

The nineteenth-century movement which is here being considered included a reemphasis on all of these points previously lifted up and also embodied the other truths which have been a fundamental part of Christianity since its beginning. It came to focus, however, in a concern beyond the individual and his personal relationship with God. The dominant theme of the Church of God movement since its inception has been the unified corporate witness of all believers. The primary concern has been the Christlike relationships within the community of Christians and a united witness to the world. In other words, this movement has distinguished itself from others in that it has included all the essential points of Christian doctrine relating to individual salvation but has made the doctrine of the church the focal point of its emphasis.

At first glance this distinction may seem of slight importance, but as one studies its total implications he comes to see that it is of supreme significance. To emphasize the necessity for personal peace with God, a personal infilling with the Holy Spirit, and a personal response to divine direction is good. The center of attention, however, in all of these points is the individual. The net result is an imbalance of concern which results in an *individualistic* approach to religion. True Christianity is always personal, but it can never be individualistic. If it is, the witness is a divided one. This kind of individualism tends to produce—and indeed has produced—many divisions in the body of Christ. But when these same truths are coupled with a strong emphasis on the corporate responsibility of individual Christians, and when each believer is brought face to face with the necessity of actualizing God's call to unity among those who follow him, then the tendencies toward division are swallowed up in a passion to be at one with other Christians in presenting a unified witness to the redemptive work of God in the world.

A great deal of the genius of this movement, then, is to be explained by the fact that, while remaining orthodox in theology, the main focus of its attention has been on the Christian community rather than on individualistic concerns. This emphasis also explains, perhaps, how the group has been saved from the pitfall of making idols of its early leaders. It undoubtedly had a great deal of influence, too, on the spirit in which these early leaders went about their task of sharing these insight with others. It was God's truth they were proclaiming and not their own. Its purpose was to promote the church and not their own organization. How could they keep from being joyful about it?

A Radical Type of Christianity

A third observation is that the Church of God reformation represents what may be called a radical approach to the Christian faith. The pioneers were not at all ashamed to be called radical. Indeed, the early issues of the *Gospel Trumpet* carried the following descriptive slogan in the masthead: "A Definite, Radical, Non-Sectarian Journal." However, these leaders did not mean that they were choosing to be extremists or fanatics. Far from it. They abhorred fanaticism and were careful to keep from being identified with extremists. By radicalism these people meant simply that they were seeking to restore the true ideals of Christianity as it was set forth in the New Testament. They were not concerned with restoring first-century Christianity in a literal sense, but they were very desirous of recapturing the essential message and spirit of the first followers of the Master.

When considered within the framework of this kind of radicalism a number of the obvious inconsistencies in the emphases of the pioneers are fully explainable. For instance, how could they make the doctrine of the church so central and yet be vigorously opposed to giving that church any structure through organization? The explanation lies in the fact that as radicals they saw the church as a spiritual, divinely structured institution. They were keenly aware that that which is essentially spiritual tends to lose its real essence if it becomes enshrouded in human forms and procedures. They were convinced that the ecclesiastical baggage which the church had acquired through the centuries had robbed it of its true character. They did not want this to happen again. As radical Christians they feared to project any organization lest the quality of the spiritual fellowship be diminished.

This failure to think in terms of developing an organization has been noted by at least one writer as a major weakness of the pioneer period in this movement. This is perhaps true in that several years passed before there was any attempt to consolidate the gains which were made. The difficulty, however, was not due to any inconsistency in their viewpoints. It was simply a matter, as Charles E. Brown says, of failing to make a distinction between organizing the church and organizing the *work* of the church. They knew they had no right to do the first, for that is the prerogative of God alone. It took some time to discover that the second was essential also if the church was to be an effective witness in the world.

The radicalism of the early leaders also explains the apparent incongruity in their approach to Christian unity. They were sometimes accused of preaching unity but promoting division by calling people to separate themselves from other Christians. It was also said that they professed fellowship with all Christians but refused to accept the testimony of those who did not fully agree with them. From the standpoint of the outsider these accusations were probably valid. The message, "Be ye separate," was strongly proclaimed, and the very certain terms in which those who failed to "walk in the light" were condemned left little doubt concerning who was and who was not out of harmony with the "truth."

In another sense, however, particularly from the viewpoint of those on the inside, there was no inconsistency in either teaching or practice. They had no interest in promoting unity on the basis of compromise. If unity were to be real and permanent it must be in line with the standard of New Testament Christianity. The church could become united only as it became holy. It could not be holy if there were unholy people in it; therefore, all true Christians should separate themselves from all their contaminating relationships. The purpose of such a stand was to draw the line of division more sharply between Christian and sinner and to erase the barrier lines between Christian and Christian.

Then too, in their refusal to fellowship others who claimed to be Christian they did not consider themselves inconsistent. A mere claim to be a Christian did not make one so; those who failed to meet the standards had already ruled themselves out of the church. The reformers were not interested in consorting with the world even if it did carry a Christian label. They drew a sharp line between professors and possessors. So, within the radical framework they were guilty of none of the charges which were hurled against them.

The fact that these people were radicals also explains why they were sometimes greatly troubled over matters which now seem to be incidental. They earnestly desired to reproduce the spirit of early Christianity, but they were not always able to distinguish between the spirit and the letter. Some tended to observe the letter in order to be sure. Thus, for almost four decades leaders in the movement were preoccupied with finding a proper interpretation of biblical admonitions regarding modest dress and outward adornment. Decisions on these points were often legalistic and sometimes ridiculous, according to modern standards, but the intention was thoroughly consistent with the ideal they had before them. The fact that later generations have become less legalistic is in no sense a criticism of these earlier leaders who were trying so desperately to be true to the New Testament standard for the church.

On the basis of these observations it becomes apparent that the Church of God reformation is closely related to its own age, is consistent with the best which has developed in the long history of Christianity, and is firmly rooted in the ideals for the church embodied in the New Testament.

Points for Discussion

1. What conditions in nineteenth-century American Christianity made religious reform necessary?

2. In what ways could the holiness movement be considered an inadequate reformation?

3. Why are reformers often accused of being heretics? Were the early leaders in the Church of God movement heretics or rebels?

4. Give a good definition of Christian radicalism. Name other groups that might qualify as radicals. Is radicalism practicable for large groups as well as small? Why or why not?

CHAPTER III

WHAT THE PIONEERS PREACHED

Almost every religious body, in order to justify its existence as a distinct group, seems compelled to declare in as specific terms as possible the way or ways in which it is different. It is usually on the basis of this distinctiveness, which is also supposed to imply superiority, that the group finds its reason for existence. Points of difference often are magnified and overemphasized in order to promote group loyalty and enthusiasm. This is the common pattern under the denominational system at present and has been so since the sixteenth century. Each group seeks to prove that its "truth" is superior to the "notions" held by others. The result is rivalry and even bitterness between the various groups even though all of them claim to be Christian.

This raises a question. Is it possible to be distinctive without being different? In the strictest sense, perhaps, the answer would have to be no, for distinctiveness implies difference. In a very practical sense, however, a person or a group could be distinctive without erecting any barriers because of difference. Distinction might well come at the point of quality—doing a better job of living up to the standards which are also taught by others, or it might come at the point of completeness— instead of picking out one or two principles of truth for emphasis, take the broadest scope of truth one can comprehend and emphasize it all. Distinctiveness of this kind need not, then, involve any differences that would function as barriers. Whatever difference exists is in degree and scope only.

"Into All the Truth"

An examination of the early preaching and writing of the Church of God reformation reveals that one of the chief points of distinctiveness among the pioneers was their desire to preach all the truth of the gospel. It was this objective, in fact, which brought the new reformation into focus in the minds of the early leaders. As early as 1878 D. S. Warner wrote: "The Lord . . . gave me a new commission to join holiness and all truth together and build up the apostolic church of the living God."

Because of this ideal there was a deliberate attempt to include all that was taught in the New Testament. The preachers neglected none of the major doctrines of the Christian faith. They preached on the love of God and also on the righteousness of God. They pictured man as a sinful creature in need of salvation and also as the special object of God's great love. They proclaimed Jesus Christ as the divine Son of God, the Savior of the world, and the healer of every disease. They emphasized the necessity of practicing the Christian ordinances of baptism, the Lord's Supper, and foot washing. They proclaimed the Bible as the Word of God and the only necessary rule of faith. In short, they wanted nothing more than to be led by the Spirit into all the truth which God had for them, and then to make this truth the content of their message to the people.

It must be kept in mind, however, that these people were reformers. There were errors and abuses which they felt needed to be corrected and important truths which they considered to be neglected. It was natural, then, that they should spend more time in dealing with these matters than they would on points where there was general agreement. A study of the themes dealt with in the early period reveals that all of the major doctrines of Christianity were included but that the subjects of chief interest were those pertaining to holiness and the nature of the church. We are now ready to consider some of these matters of particular interest. Each may be stated in scriptural terms.

"The God of Peace Sanctify You Wholly" (1 Thess. 5:23)

One of the first principles set forth by these nineteenth-century reformers was that every genuine Christian ought to live a life that is holy. The holy life was defined as one free from outward sin and also free from any inward intention to do wrong. That they expected all within their fellowship to live up to the standard is evidenced by the fact that from the beginning they spoke of themselves as "the saints." This was not a title to be attached to a select few of the holy people of the past but a descriptive term applying to the living company of those who, here and now, were fully controlled by the Holy Spirit.

Such a state could not be achieved by purely natural means, however. Even as it was impossible for man to be redeemed except as he accepted the supernatural work of God through Jesus Christ, so also it was not possible for a person to live a holy life in his own strength. He must have supernatural assistance, and this was available when one would take a second step in his spiritual experience and accept the sanctifying work of the Holy Spirit.

The importance of the doctrine of sanctification in the minds of the pioneers can hardly be overexaggerated. If a single truth were to be designated as the basic root from which the reformation sprang, this would probably be considered most basic. Many sermons, articles, and tracts expounded this truth at great length. D. S. Warner began his editorial career in 1878 when he was put in charge of the holiness department of the *Herald of Gospel Freedom.* His first book, published in 1880 before there was a *Gospel Trumpet,* was entitled, *Bible Proofs of a Second Work of Grace.* It was through contacts made in the preaching of this doctrine that many of the early leaders in the Church of God reformation were brought together.

In the early writing and preaching on sanctification two points stand out clearly. The first is that sanctification is a divine work, wrought by the Holy Spirit, and that it alters a person's very nature. It is not something which persons can do for themselves, so it cannot be identified with the blessing one receives in making a deeper consecration or a more complete submission to the divine will. The second point is that sanctification is a complete work. Entire sanctification meant an elevation of life to the plane that even one's motives and desires were made perfect and were brought into harmony with the will of God. This did not preclude growth in knowledge and understanding nor improvement in conduct, for these would continue as long as one lived, but it did demand a life that was free from any carnal intention.

"Be Not Conformed to This World" (Rom. 12:2)

The doctrine of holiness was not an abstract theological concept to these early leaders; it was a practical standard for everyday living. Positively, holiness was defined as a life under the complete direction of the Holy Spirit. Negatively it was defined as nonconformity to the world. This required that *worldliness* be defined. The pioneers were very practical minded, and so they were not content with a general definition. They sought to be specific so they named particular practices and procedures which were considered worldly and were to be avoided by the saints. In general, the items included were of the same nature as the ascetic disciplines imposed by other Christian groups greatly concerned about personal piety. The chief areas in which definitions seemed necessary were those of food, dress, amusements, and relationships to society.

It is neither possible nor necessary at this point to enumerate all the items which were included in these definitions. Partaking of certain foods and beverages was declared to be wrong because they were considered harmful to the body. It was on this basis that tea and coffee were under condemnation for a number of years. Because tight-fitting corsets were considered injurious to health they were also condemned. The majority of the regulations involving dress were attempts to avoid any indications of vanity or pride. During the early 1900s women were asked to forego lace and ruffles, and the men were expected to leave off their neckties. The wearing of gold and other ornaments was considered worldly adornment. Most forms of professional entertainment were regarded as sinful, and anything more than a mild interest in public affairs was considered an overconcern with the things of this world.

While most of the regulations were based on scriptural injunctions and sound reasoning it cannot be denied that at times fanaticism was prevalent. At lease some of the early leaders, however, were careful to keep the movement free from extremism. D. S. Warner, for instance, writing in the May 1, 1884, issue of the *Gospel Trumpet,* refers to a minister who was being persecuted because he had some fancy portraits of his family made. Warner leaves no room for doubt regarding his own attitude. "All such judging from outward appearances and mere trifles," he wrote, "is not of God, but of the devil. . . . The old Pharisees that 'strain at a gnat and swallow a camel' are not dead yet."

A backward look at some of these matters may provoke a few smiles and may even make one wonder why there was so much concern over seemingly small matters. To these people, however, such standards were far from being small matters. They were seeking a tangible means of indicating their separation from the world. These were the marks of distinction that would help them convey their witness. They were earnest and sincere men and women who wanted more than anything else to be faithful to their high calling as children of God. The standards and disciplines which they imposed upon themselves were born out of a deep conviction that these were necessary in order to be true to God's demands.

"Come Out . . . and Be Ye Separate" (2 Cor. 6:17)

The early leaders of the Church of God reformation were sometimes called "come-outers" because they advocated the withdrawal of all true Christians from the various sects and denominations in which they were scattered and divided. These pioneers believed it was possible to reconstitute the church of the New Testament by inviting all who had been spiritually reborn to enter into a fellowship which was not restricted by any of the organizational or creedal limitations which had been established by the existing churches. One of the early congregations drew up a resolution which declared, "We adhere to no body or organization but the church of God, bought by the blood of Christ, organized by the Holy Spirit, and governed by the Bible."

In taking such a stand these people were careful to make it clear that they were not starting another sect. Their intention was quite to the contrary. They, indeed, were providing an escape from sectism. Instead of organizing another "church among the churches" they were issuing a call to all true Christians to shake off the secondary allegiances which were keeping them apart and to join in this movement to restore the church to its intended purity and unity.

For scriptural support for "come-outism," the early leaders found many Old Testament warnings that Israel should avoid contamination by their idol-worshiping neighbors. In the New Testament Paul quotes one of these passages (Isa. 52:11) and uses it to admonish the Corinthians to keep themselves free from the sinful paganism with which they were surrounded. To the pioneers of the Church of God reformation these Scripture passages were perfectly applicable. Sectism was sin. It was to be forsaken just like anything else sinful. One could not be genuinely Christian and participate in this sinful division of the body of Christ. The only logical course was to "come out" from these ungodly sectarian organizations into the true church of God.

"The Lord Added to the Church" (Acts 2:47)

Pioneer leaders of the Church of God movement were convinced that the various systems of church joining allowed many unworthy people to become affiliated with what was supposed to be a divine institution. They searched the Scriptures for clear guidance as to the proper method for admitting people into the church. They found no procedure outlined and no method recommended, but they did find that the church is a divine institution. The more they studied, the more apparent it became that no one has the right to set the boundaries of the church. Neither is it the right of any person or any group to declare who is in or who is out of the church. God alone can do that. Church membership procedures, then, are nothing more than humanly devised ceremonies and have little or no relationship to real membership in the church.

In order to avoid the error of presuming to do God's judging for him these reformers declared that one becomes a member of the church when he experiences the new birth. No rite or ceremony is necessary to admit one into the divine fellowship. As soon as one's sins are forgiven, he at that moment enters the brotherhood of the redeemed. The genuineness of that conversion experience is a matter for God alone to decide. The visible fellowship is made up of all those who testify that this divine work has been accomplished in their own souls. This truth is well expressed in the words of a song written in 1923 by C. W. Naylor.

The day of sects and creeds for us forevermore is past,
Our brotherhood are all the saints upon the world so vast;
We reach our hands in fellowship to every blood-washed one,
While love entwines about each heart in which God's will is done.

"Now Hath God Set the Members . . . in the Body" (1 Cor. 12:18)

One of the most apparent aspects of the early preaching in the Church of God movement was the horror which the leaders had for all types of humanly devised organization in the church. There were two reasons why they felt this way. The first was a continuation of their belief that the church was a divine institution and was not subject to human structuring. The second was a burning conviction that the Holy Spirit had been designated as the full governing agency of the church and any attempt at "man rule" was sheer interference with the divine plan.

Looking back on this period from the vantage point of the

present we might wonder why these people were so afraid of organization. As one examines the sermons and writings of the leaders, however, he discovers that they had a very clear understanding of the real nature of the church's difficulties. They could see that many of the barriers existing between Christians were due to the fact that each group followed after its own peculiar notions and developed loyalty to its own system rather than to Christ alone. They also could see that practically none of the organizational systems left much room for the operation of the Holy Spirit.

Their real fear, then, was not of organization as such but of humanly devised organization without the control of the Holy Spirit. To keep from falling into the error of "man rule" they resolved to develop no system of their own to which people might attach their allegiance and to keep all organization at a minimum. This, they felt, would give the Holy Spirit opportunity to work more directly and accomplish his will more completely since there was no highly developed system to get in the way.

The principle on which these pioneers were operating was basically right. The church is not a human institution, and it cannot be humanly organized. The fact that they were not at first able to see the difference between organizing the church, which they had no right to do, and organizing the cooperative work of the people of God who compose the church, which was their responsibility to do, undoubtedly caused needless problems and perhaps allowed for more losses than necessary. Even so, the ideal which they upheld was solid truth from which there must be no departure.

"That They May All Be One" (John 17:21)

It might at first seem that all these points of special emphasis were unrelated to each other and even incidental to the central truth of the Christian gospel which is obviously that God sent his Son into the world to save sinners. Upon closer examination, however, it is discovered that all of these point directly to this central truth, in that all of them are concerned with the characteristics of the company of the redeemed—the church. To these five truths the pioneers added another great affirmation which brought their whole message into sharper focus. This crowning emphasis was the firm conviction that God intended for all his people to be united in one fellowship.

This meant that the early leaders were not content to point to the error and sin of division. They did not stop with an invitation to "come out" of the sects. They went a step further and sought to demonstrate that a real visible unity of the church was an achievable ideal. The accomplishment of this goal, they said, could never be reached by applying external pressures, by developing a super organization, or by compromising differences. It was possible only as people were brought together by sharing in the common experience of redemption through Jesus Christ, were willing to open themselves to all truth, and measured their lives according to their full understanding of the will of God. A unity achieved on this basis would be true and genuine, for it would grow out of a real unity of spirit rather than being some kind of union imposed upon people who were not really together at heart.

The Church of God reformation movement was more than a series of emphases, however. It was a crusade to open the door of all truth. Some of the specific content of this truth was lifted up and proclaimed, but the limits of truth were never defined. That was left open, for God was still at work among his people, and who could say when the boundaries of his revelation had been reached?

Points for Discussion

1. What did the pioneers mean by "entire sanctification"?
2. How may one show his separateness from the world?
3. Is the "sin of sectism" as serious now as when the early leaders in the Church of God reformation began preaching against it?
4. What are some of the dangers in church-joining procedures?
5. Explain the difference between organizing the church and organizing the work of the church.

CHAPTER IV

SPREADING THE TRUTH

Ideas and beliefs are tremendously important in shaping the character of a movement, but they do not of themselves automatically set the movement in motion. Things begin to happen only as individuals become convinced of the importance of their beliefs and are fired with a passion to actualize and propagate the truths which have been formulated. This is what it took to bring the Church of God reformation into being. The story of the early development of this movement is the story of men and women captivated by the spirit of truth and impelled by the belief that they were the instruments for a more complete fulfillment of the will of God.

Bold but Not Hasty

It has already been noted that almost four years elapsed between the time (January 1878) when Warner first received his "new commission to join holiness and all truth together," and those dramatic events at Beaver Dam, Indiana, and Carson City, Michigan, in October of 1881. These certainly were not drastic spur-of-the-moment actions without careful consideration of all the implications involved. It was also in 1878 that another of the early leaders, A. J. Kilpatrick, first began to "see the light." In leaving the United Brethren church he declared, "Every person who has salvation and belongs to a denominational church belongs to two, and Jesus built only one church and said that the gates of hell should not prevail against it." Warner and Kilpatrick met in Payne, Ohio, in 1879 and discovered that their views were almost identical. It is reported that at this meeting each man renounced his sectarian ordination to the ministry and then each in turn ordained the other. This was a perfect setting for announcing the launching of a new movement, but no such announcement was made. Warner also had conversations with various others, such as J. C. Fisher and his wife Allie, Jeremiah

Cole, and W. J. Henry, but none of these contacts resulted in any premature action.

Part of the reason for this delay in getting started was undoubtedly the lack of any clear direction concerning the proper action to take. They did not want to be accused of starting another sect, and they were reluctant to disrupt what little harmony there was within and among the various churches. As time went on, though, they became convinced that unity within the framework of the sectarian system was an impossibility. Furthermore, they were certain that the time had arrived when God was calling his people out of this sinful system. So they took the bold step and declared themselves free from all man-made sects and members only of the one holy church of God. Once this definite break had been made there was no longer any hesitancy to speak or to act. Fearlessly they declared their position wherever they could find an audience, and without apology they called upon all true Christians to abandon the sects in which they were scattered so they might participate in the pure fellowship of the redeemed without restrictions.

As the full implications of this message began to be realized, those who had seen "the light on the church" could hardly contain themselves for the sheer joy of having such a revelation in their possession. They could not wait to tell others about it. Within a matter of months they were employing all the techniques then known to broadcast the message. They took every opportunity to give their personal witness, they held public meetings in almost every conceivable place, they published literature and sent it out by the ton, they wrote songs and taught people to sing them, and they seldom waited for an invitation to give their testimony. They had a story to tell, and they were determined that as many people as possible should hear it.

A "Flying Ministry"

None of the pioneer leaders thought in terms of establishing a headquarters as a base of operations. Each felt his own responsibility to tell the message to as many people as possible in the shortest time. Instead of congregating in one place to build a holy community, almost all of the early preachers became traveling evangelists who went from place to place proclaiming their message. They referred to their work as a "flying ministry."

It would be quite impossible, of course, even to name all those who had a part in the work in those early years. No ministerial lists were even attempted until the early 1900s and then only for the purpose of providing the necessary credentials for obtaining clergy rates on the railroads. Except for those who sent in regular reports of their activities to the *Gospel Trumpet* there is little record for the first twenty years of the several hundreds who went about preaching and singing the message which had come to mean so much to them. The few who are mentioned here are simply illustrative of the many more who heard the call of God and responded with a full dedication of their time and energy to the work of spreading the truth.

Any listing of the early evangelists should probably begin with the name of D. S. Warner. Although neither he nor any other single individual can properly be called the founder of this reformation he is generally regarded, because of his abilities as a powerful preacher and gifted writer and also because of his position as first editor of the *Gospel Trumpet,* as a key figure in the early days of the movement.

After the eventful day in 1881 when he declared himself free from all sectarian divisions, his real ministry began. In his remaining fifteen years he traveled and preached in almost every section of the United States and in parts of Canada. Despite the frailty of his body he endured hardships that would have stopped many of much hardier stock. Along with this heavy travel schedule he continued to edit the *Gospel Trumpet,* to write articles, tracts, books, songs, and poems, and to keep up with a variety of other interests. Until his death in 1895 at the comparatively early age of fifty-three he was unquestionably the central figure in the movement to which he gave his best. His fearless witness regarding the purity and unity of the church makes this humble man of God one of the great spiritual leaders of all time.

The movement was by no means a one-man affair, however. Within a matter of months the score or so of preachers mentioned earlier were on the road. Kilpatrick was busy in Ohio and the Fishers in Michigan. Michels, Speck, and Palmer traveled together as a team for about two years and then each continued to evangelize on his own. Jeremiah Cole was joined by his brother George and his sister Mary in Missouri. William G. Schell was added to the workers from Ohio and Charles Koonce assisted Clayton in Pennsylvania.

By the late 1880s a large number of new leaders joined the ranks of messengers who traveled, preached, sang, and wrote. The most notable of these, perhaps, was Enoch E. Byrum, an Indiana farm boy who interrupted his college education in 1887 to become business manager of the Gospel Trumpet publishing work which by then was located in Grand Junction, Michigan. He was later to become the second editor of the company's publications and played a large role in the movement's development. His brother, Noah H. Byrum, was also enlisted as a worker and later became treasurer of the company. Other leaders of note who joined the work before 1890 were James Pine, A. B. Stanberry, George Bolds and four of his children who became preachers in Missouri; Lodema Kaser in Indiana; Dr. G. R. Achor and Dr. S. G. Bryant, two medical doctors in Kansas who turned evangelists; William Hartman, Adelbert Bixler, and Leroy Sheldon in Michigan; John E. Roberts in Colorado; Andrew Byers, his two sons Jacob W. and Andrew L., and Abram Bixler from Illinois; and many others. An editorial report in the *Gospel Trumpet* of evangelistic activities in 1888 concluded with the observation: "Many are running to and fro. Amen."

In taking their stand for the "truth" and answering a call to the ministry these men and women almost without exception cut themselves off from any sure means of livelihood. Several of them were already ministers in various denominations, some had been public school teachers, some were farmers, and some had been in other professions. All of these occupations provided adequate incomes, but reformation preachers had no guarantees whatever. Theirs was entirely a ministry of faith. Seldom were they able even to schedule meetings far in advance, for most of the calls were direct leads from one place to another. On more than one occasion a minister closed a meeting without sufficient train fare to get to his next appointment. The amounts sent home to support families were often meager and almost always inadequate. Even so, a sufficient amount usually came in to keep the work going without interruption, and the needed help for families always seemed to come from somewhere. On many occasions these matters were the subjects of earnest prayer.

Many of these ministers exercised their faith in still another important way by going to hold meetings in places where they had no contacts and no assurance of even a place to sleep. On occasion their faith was rewarded, but there were times when no bed was provided except a cornfield or the benches of the schoolhouse where the meeting was being held.

During the summer months it was not even necessary to find a building. It was common practice to hold meetings in tents, in brush arbors, in groves, and on the streets of towns and cities. The most common outdoor meeting place was in a grove where planks had been laid across stumps or rocks for benches and almost any kind of table or stand served as a pulpit. For longer meetings the camp-meeting technique, long used by other groups, was quickly adopted by the pioneers and became standard practice. The earliest extant issue of the *Gospel Trumpet* contains notices of several such meetings for the summer of 1881. These open-air meetings usually created considerable interest and often were the means of inciting opposition and persecution.

When the weather was unfit for outdoor meetings there was always the problem of finding a suitable place to hold services, for the movement had not yet progressed far enough to have buildings. The most common meeting place probably was in private homes. When the crowds got too large to be accommodated they would find a larger place. In many instances they secured the loan of other church buildings, and then preached to the people that they should come out of the sect which owned the building! Sometimes they would secure permission to use country schoolhouses, courthouses, vacant store buildings, skating rinks, and even granaries and barns. The surroundings did not matter; the important thing was that people be given the opportunity to hear the message.

Tons of Literature

Along with their preaching these traveling evangelists distributed literature. At first this consisted chiefly of copies of the *Gospel Trumpet,* the biweekly paper which Warner edited. Later it included tracts and books published by the Gospel Trumpet Company. Without minimizing the influence of the many powerful sermons which were preached it can still be said that the printed word was probably the most significant instrument in spreading the message of the Church of God reformation. The literature reached farther and contacted more people than the evangelists themselves were ever able to do in public meetings.

The story of the *Gospel Trumpet* is a fascinating one, and the record of its successes and failures is almost the record of the movement itself. For the first five years the survival of the paper was an open question, and on more than one occasion the answer seemed more likely to be no than yes. In the words of H. C. Wickersham, "The outfit was a very small affair." The first two issues were printed at Rome City, Indiana, but Warner moved what little equipment there was to Indianapolis early in 1881. Here the office was moved several times, finally ending up in the editor's kitchen. The prospect of a better location brought a move to Cardington, Ohio, in the fall of 1882, and the following spring another move was made to Bucyrus, Ohio, twenty miles away. The year spent there was a tragic one for Warner, for he met with strong opposition to the work in which he was engaged. Among those who opposed him was his own wife. She did not accompany him when he moved the *Trumpet* to Williamston, Michigan, in April of 1884.

In Michigan the publishing work began to get on its feet. After two years the office was moved to Grand Junction where it stayed for twelve years. Other moves to Moundsville, West Virginia, in 1898 and to Anderson, Indiana, in 1906 were made primarily to meet the demands of substantial growth.

More important than either the location or the equipment, however, was the material which was turned out on the company's presses. The *Gospel Trumpet* became the medium through which all the workers could keep in touch with each other, thus giving solidarity to a movement which might have soon spent itself in small isolated groups. It contained articles designed to instruct those recently enlisted in the movement and to enrich the understanding of those who were seeking for more truth. Copies of this paper were distributed widely, both through the mail and by handing them to people on the street, on trains, and in waiting rooms. In Williamston the company published its first book—a songbook. Some tracts were also printed there. After the move to Grand Junction many more tracts and booklets were published. More books also began to come from the presses. In January, 1892, the *Gospel Trumpet* became a weekly.

At times complaints arose that literature was being wasted because tons of printed material were distributed free of charge. When one considers the results, however, such complaints hardly seem justified. It is difficult to find a single area to which the movement has spread that was not first made aware of this reformation by some piece of literature published by the Gospel Trumpet Company.

Singing the Truth

It would be hard to overestimate the significance of music in the spread of the movement in the early days. Warner himself was a composer of both music and lyrics and he also loved to sing. Many of the other early leaders had musical talents, too. It was no accident that the first book the company published was a songbook, *Songs of Victory*. By 1900 four other songbooks had been issued. Most of the songs included were new and were written to fit the ideals and ideas of the movement. In the words of J. C. Fisher, editor of that first songbook, these songs were an expression of "the glorious light of liberty, grace, truth, and power the free and holy church has attained in this blessed evening light."

In 1886, the year following the appearance of *Songs of Victory,* Warner instituted a new evangelistic technique, the "company." This consisted of a party of four to six people who traveled as a team of workers. The most obvious advantage of this arrangement was that it provided a group of singers. Warner's first company, consisting of Barney Warren, Nannie Kigar, Frances Miller, and "Mother" Sarah Smith, traveled together for over four years. Many other evangelists procured singers and organized their own companies. It might be noted in passing that this system provided an excellent opportunity for many young women to become active in evangelistic work.

One of the standard procedures was to drive into a town in a buggy or spring wagon, singing with all the strength the company would muster. They would drive up and down the streets of the town until a sufficient crowd had gathered to make an announcement about the meeting they were about to begin. In such a way they were able to attract many people who would not otherwise have attended. Many stories are told of singing in hotel lobbies, railroad stations, and other public gathering places.

More important than the fact that the early leaders were interested in music is the additional fact that the songs they composed were in truth lyrical expressions of the message they proclaimed. Titles like "The Church Triumphant," "Brighter Days Are Sweetly Dawning," "He Sanctifies Me," and

"There's Music in My Soul" are loaded with theological overtones. Those who failed to respond to the spoken word often were led to make a commitment when the same message was set to music and sung by competent singers.

Innovative Enthusiasm

Accounts of the evangelistic zeal of these early leaders reveal they were not only vigorously active, they were also creatively inventive in devising ways to reach new people. One of the best examples of this is a venture which was called the "Floating Bethel." In 1893 George Clayton purchased a large river barge docked on the Allegheny River in Pennsylvania. He brought it down to Pittsburg and there had it rennovated and had a chapel and living quarters for several people built on its flat deck. His plan was to enlist a number of workers to join him and they would float this unpowered craft down the Ohio River to the Mississippi and then on to the Gulf, stopping at every town on both sides of the river to hold evangelistic meetings. The "Bethel" left Pittsburg in early 1894 and continued its downriver mission for over four years with many wonderful and challenging experiences and a few near tragic mishaps. It caught fire and burned in Moundsville, West Virginia before Clayton's dream was completely fulfilled, but in the process of its slow journey it had utilized the services of many important leaders, including D. S. Warner and Herbert M. Riggle, and had been the vehicle for planting more than a dozen congregations along the Ohio River in Pennsylvania and West Virginia.

Workers Together

In addition to the evangelists and singers many other people had a part in sending out the message. Many people who never felt a call to the ministry and who remained at their places of employment witnessed effectively by personal testimony and by passing out literature. Still others, who were called "gospel workers," gave assistance to evangelists in revival meetings and ministered to people's spiritual needs as they had opportunity.

Then there was the Trumpet Family, those faithful folk who worked at the publishing house without pay, some of them for many years. All of these had an important part in spreading the truth and making a movement out of the truth which had been revealed.

Points for Discussion

1. What were some of the factors which kept the leaders in the Church of God reformation from making a break with the denominations any sooner than they did?
2. What were some of the strong points of the "flying ministry" technique of evangelism? What are some of the weaknesses of this method?
3. Describe some of the hardships faced by those who pioneered in developing the Church of God movement.
4. Cite some illustrations of how literature proved to be an effective means of evangelism.
5. What were some of the specific functions performed by the *Gospel Trumpet* in the early development of the movement?
6. It has been said, "The Church of God has been a singing people." What are some of the implications of this statement?

CHAPTER V

INTO ALL THE WORLD

For the first several years the evangelistic efforts of the Church of God reformation leaders were confined largely to the United States. The calls from various parts of the country were so numerous and the workers were so few that there was little time to think in terms of sending ministers to other parts of the world. It was not long, however, until contacts were made, largely through the *Gospel Trumpet,* and calls began to come from other nations.

Canada

As might be expected, the first of these international contacts was in Canada. As early as 1882 a woman in Ontario by the name of Eliza White was reading the *Gospel Trumpet.* In later correspondence she asked that Warner come to Canada to help in the work which she started. It was not until November of 1888, however, that Warner and his evangelistic company went to Ontario. They stayed there until March, 1889, holding revivals in several localities. From one of these places Warner reported: "We . . . had not much idea of the stage of progress the work had attained here. But we are happy to say that we found more dear saints here than we had expected."

While in Canada Warner was able to be of great assistance in giving instruction to the local leaders and in helping them work out some difficulties which had arisen. After his departure the way was then open for others to cross the border and work in this new field. The two couples who contributed most to the development of the Canadian church in the next decade were the George T. Claytons and the J. A. Dillons. W. J. Henry and A. J. Kilpatrick also held meetings in Ontario. The efforts of these and others were coupled with the work of local leaders like William Deakman, John E. Smith, David Moyer, J. C.

Blaney, Emma Tufford, Ethel Williams, Harry Nelson, and others. By 1899 the work in eastern Canada was sufficiently strong to form a base for several functioning congregations. The earliest of these were in Welland, Grand Bend, Fenwick, Dashwood, and London. Later leaders included George H. Pye, J. E. Campbell, W. H. Schroeder, H. French Wilson, Albert Boelke, Glenn Beach, and Arthur Kreuger. By 1975 there were ten congregations in Ontario with a total membership of nearly 600.

In western Canada the beginning of the work was somewhat later but it developed more extensively. As early as 1905 Hiram A. Brooks, who had been ministering in Ontario, visited relatives in Saskatchewan and initiated a work in the city of Saskatoon. That same year W. H. Smith, a black minister from Denver, went to Edmonton, Alberta and started a mission. The next year a German language congregation was started in Winnipeg by Karl Arbeiter from North Dakota, and Louis Neff from Colorado held meetings in Ferintosh and several other cities in Alberta. From 1908 to 1918 the most active minister in western Canada was Leonard E. Millensifer who moved from Nebraska to a homestead near Edmonton in 1905. After attending one of W. H. Smith's meetings he dedicated his life to Christ and the ministry of the Church of God. In a decade of intense evangelism amid the rigors of a pioneer land he traversed the provinces of western Canada preaching in both English and German. Pastorates in Saskatoon, Edmonton, and Calgary provided bases for further outreach. A breakdown in health forced curtailment of activity for several years, but he returned to serve in the late 1920s and continued on a reduced schedule until his death in 1948.

Others who ministered significantly in western Canada would include Reuben W. May, George Monroe, J. S. Walkof, Harry C. Gardner, Henry C. Heffren, and A. D. Semrau. Three long-term missionaries, G. P. Tasker, Irene Engst, and Lydia Hansen, have come from the area. By 1975 there were thirty-five congregations in the western provinces.

Mexico

The first extension of the Church of God beyond the southern border of the United States also came quite early. B. F. Elliott of Santa Barbara, California became greatly concerned about the Mexican people. He learned the Spanish language and in 1891 went to Baja, California where he won some converts and established a publishing work in the city of La Paz. Several years later, in 1908, the D. W. Pattersons joined the Elliots and prospects for further expansion were bright. Rumors of revolutions, however, forced both families to leave and the work was not sufficiently strong to survive their departure.

The threatened revolution did come in 1910 and one of the measures growing out of the new political regime was a prohibition for any minister from a foreign country to preach or hold services in any building in Mexico. This stopped all foreign missionary work and it was almost two decades before another continuing witness in Mexico could be established. A. T. Maciel, a Mexican national who had been converted in California and entered the ministry in 1928, was able to make periodic trips into Mexico and hold evangelistic meetings. One of his converts was A. E. Valez, a tailor in Reynosa, who responded to God's call and became a minister. Valez was instrumental in starting a congregation in San Antonio de las Alazanas in 1933. Sixteen years later this congregation dedicated the first church building erected by the Church of God in Mexico. The second building was completed in 1951 at Jame where a congregation had been worshiping in homes since 1934. By 1975 a total of twenty-five congregations were functioning in seven Mexican states.

The solid growth of the Mexican work is closely related to the development of the Saltillo Bible Training Center, *La Buena Tierra,* which held its first classes in 1954 with Maurice Caldwell as the director. Young men and women receive training in this school and go out to become pastors and leaders of the congregations that are established. Through an extension department, classes are provided for pastors and lay persons in the villages and cities where they reside, thus strengthening the leadership of older congregations as well as new ones. Since 1972 the school has had a Mexican director and more nationals are assuming responsibility in educational leadership.

The British Isles

After 1893 the Church of God reformation became more and more international in its outlook. The number of those whose interests extended beyond the seas increased year by year. In 1894 D. S. Warner expressed a desire to make a trip all the way around the world for the purpose of preaching the message and finding suitable locations for futher evangelistic work. Although he was not able to carry out his wish, it was not just a fanciful dream, for already others were in the process of doing the very things he had planned.

Expansion of the reformation message beyond the oceans was first to England. The initial impetus for this venture seems to have come from W. J. Henry. In a testimony printed in the *Gospel Trumpet* (January 12, 1893) he tells how in the spring of 1892 he was led to make a deeper and more complete consecration. Included in this was a specific consecration to "go to foreign fields if the Lord would call you, and you would get a letter to go, and the means would be furnished." He told some of his brethren about this, he says, "but they laughed and said there was enough work to be done at home." In December of that year, however, he did get a letter (he does not say from whom) and the means was provided. On January 7, 1893, he and George R. Achor sailed for Liverpool.

It was not the intention of Henry and Achor to remain long in England, for they fully expected to go on to the "dark countries." By March, however, they were convinced that the Lord would have them stay there and take advantage of the opportunities which were opening to them. Later that same year J. H. and Mrs. Rupert, J. W. Daugherty, and Lena Shoffner crossed the Atlantic and assisted in the growing work in

England. In the next few years an increasing number of evangelists went from America to work in the British Isles or to preach there a short time as they were en route to other places. Among these were W. H. Cheatham, C. E. Orr, Jennie C. Rutty, E. E. Byrum, G. P. Tasker, C. J. Blewitt, A. D. Khan, E. A. Reardon, F. G. Smith, and H. M. Riggle. Adam Allan worked for many years in Scotland and Ireland. William Hopwood became the leader of a congregation in Birkenhead, England, just across the river from Liverpool. In 1921 Allan and Hopwood began publishing a British *Gospel Trumpet* which was continued until Hopwood's death in 1948. John Larmour succeeded Hopwood at Birkenhead and maintained some oversight of a congregation in Liverpool and one in Belfast, Ireland. In the mid 1960s a new interracial congregation, composed mostly of emigrants from Commonwealth countries, was launched in London with some initial support from the Missionary Board in the United States and from congregations of the Church of God in the Caribbean area.

The Continent of Europe

The first direct contact with Europe apparently was made by J. H. and Hattie Rupert who went to Hamburg, Germany, from England around the year 1894. They remained in Germany for about eight months and raised up a small congregation. After the Rupert's departure the congregation ceased to function after a time, but some of the people remained faithful and were instrumental in helping to get the work started again about a decade later.

The real beginning of the work on the Continent was around 1903. George Vielguth, a German-speaking minister from Kansas, held several meetings in Germany from 1901 to 1902, reviving interest among those who had been contacted earlier as well as making several new contacts. When he returned to America in 1902 he aroused the interest of several other German-speaking brethren. The following year he and several more preachers went back to Germany and were successful in establishing congregations in several places. Those most active in this work were Karl Arbeiter, Otto Doebert, William Ebel, and Vielguth.

From Germany the reformation movement spread to Switzerland, Holland, Poland, Latvia, and Russia. The work in the Scandinavian countries came later and was largely the result of labors by Scandinavian people in the United States who went back to their native countries as evangelists. The earliest of these missionaries to their homeland were Nels Renbeck and Morris Johnson in Denmark and Carl Forsberg and O. T. Ring in Sweden. They began this work around 1909 to 1910. The beginning of World War I forced most of these American workers to leave Europe, but by then the work was quite firmly established.

The subsequent growth of the Church of God in Europe came largely without assistance from America, except for some aid in rehabilitation following World War II. West Germany became the center for vigorous growth and solid development. A publishing work was established in Essen and a Bible school for the training of leaders was developed in Fritzlar. By 1975 there were more than eighty congregations and preaching points. In Switzerland, which is closely associated with the German work, there are four congregations. Holland has one large congregation at Waubach and several smaller meeting groups. In Denmark there are four congregations, a small Bible school, and a modest publishing work. Greece has one congregation in Athens which is small in size but has an excellent building. In East Europe the status of the Church of God has been largely unknown to westerners since the close of World War II, but reports indicate both survival and growth. It is known that several groups are meeting in East Germany, that there are more than thirty functioning congregations in Russia, five in Hungary, four in Bulgaria, and an unknown number in Rumania and Poland. The newest European expansion is in Italy where, in 1973, a work was started in Ostia, near Rome, by the Franco Santonocitos who had been led to Christ through the work of the

Church of God youth center in Alexandria, Egypt. By 1975 plans were laid for establishing a second congregation in another community.

India, Bangladesh, and Southern Asia

The first extension of the Church of God reformation to a non-Christian land was in the closing years of the nineteenth century when contacts were established in India. In 1895 a young man by the name of A. D. Khan, a converted Muslim, was attending the University of Calcutta. He was anxious to learn more about the Christian faith which he had so recently embraced, so he read all the literature he could find which pertained to Christianity. Among some samples from American publishers of religious books he found a catalog from the Gospel Trumpet Company. He liked the advertisements, so he sent for some of the books. He found that they taught what he had already come to believe through his own study of the New Testament. He enlisted some friends and they began to hold meetings in Calcutta.

In 1897 India was struck by a severe famine. Stories of the great suffering of the people were carried in American newspapers, and many individuals and groups were moved to send relief to the starving. Many people associated with the Church of God desired to join in this good work, and a considerable sum was raised. Gorham Tufts, Jr., of Chicago, was chosen to carry this gift to India and to supervise its distribution. He made contact with Khan at that time. Tufts returned to America in October and gave a favorable report of the work Khan was doing. Within a short time over half a ton of books and tracts was sent to India for distribution, as well as two small printing presses for publishing more gospel literature. Khan used them to good advantage. Before any missionaries from America arrived he and two other capable leaders, J. J. M. Roy and M. Moses, had laid a good foundation for future work.

In 1903 Khan visited the United States and traveled

extensively among the churches. This trip marked a turning point in the outlook and vision of the whole movement. A world consciousness had been in process for over ten years, but Khan's visit brought it to full birth. When he returned to India the following year E. E. Byrum, the editor of the *Gospel Trumpet,* the G. W. Baileys of Washington, and Evelyn Nichols of Idaho went with him. Byrum stayed in India for a few weeks and then continued on his round-the-world tour. The Bailey's remained for a year. Evelyn Nichols married J. J. M. Roy and continued to live and work in India. Other early missionaries included Andrew Shiffler, the Robert Jarvises, V. C. Maiden and his family, the G. P. Taskers, Lottie Theobald, Thaddeus Neff, and Josephine McCrie. Centers were established at Cuttack, Lahore, Calcutta, and several points in the province of Assam.

In Travancore in South India there was also a contact established around the turn of the century. P. J. Philip was a member of a small group of Christians who were seeking a more vital faith than they found in the established church. A stranger told him of a religious paper which proclaimed the same things this group believed. In this way contact was made with the *Gospel Trumpet* and with A. D. Khan, who visited Travancore several times. A solid work was established by Philip without the aid of missionaries from America. It was not until after World War II that anyone went from the United States to asssist in this work.

Beginning around 1918 another center for mission activity was developed in East Bengal at Lalmanirhat by the F. W. Heinlys. They were later followed by the Robert Clarks and still later by the Paul Hutchins. This was a Muslim region and the normally slow progress was made even more difficult by political problems. When India was partitioned in 1947 this territory became East Pakistan. The civil war of 1971 separated this eastern province and it became the new country of Bangladesh. The Hutchins were on furlough at the time of the war and they were not allowed to resume their service. After local leaders returned from a brief exile in India they reestablished the church and the primary school, so the work continued without the assistance of missionaries from overseas.

In a period of almost seventy years the Church of God sent more than forty missionaries to India, some of them spending almost a lifetime of service there. By 1972, however, the stage of the development of the church and some of the proscriptive political regulations regarding foreigners in India made it apparent that the time had come to withdraw all missionary personnel. When the Sidney Johnsons left on furlough in that year the church in India knew they would not be returning. But the church was ready for independence. Three strong centers of work had developed: in the central area comprising West Bengal and Orissa, in the state of Meghalaya in northeast India, and in Kerala State in South India. The total membership was about 18,000 Christians.

After their 1973 furlough the Sidney Johnsons went to Bangkok, Thailand to be in a location sufficiently close to be of service to the churches in India, Bangladesh, and the Philippines should they be needed. The resultant missionary presence proved beneficial and also had an unanticipated further development—the beginning of a new base for Christian witness in Thailand with possible outreach to other countries in Southeast Asia.

The Caribbean Area

The next outpost of the Church of God reformation was in the West Indies. In 1906 the George H. Pyes, Lydia Yoder, and N. S. Duncan went to Trinidad. By 1909 there was a sufficiently strong work to leave it in the hands of native workers for about two years. J. Frank Shaw went to the islands in 1911 and remained until 1925. Many other missionaries, including the A. E. Rathers, the Thaddeus Neffs, the Herman Smiths and the Donald Johnsons, served in Trinidad and on the neighboring islands of Tobago and Grenada. By 1975 there were some twenty-five congregations on these islands, and a well developed West Indies Bible Institute was operated completely by local leadership.

N. S. Duncan preached on the island of Barbados as early as 1906 but it was not until 1912 that an ongoing work was established. Missionaries gave assistance until 1962 when all mission properties were turned over to the General Assembly of the Church of God in Barbados and the church began functioning under the leadership of national pastors. A total of nineteen congregations have developed.

In 1907 the George W. Olsons and their daughter Mary began work in Jamaica in response to an appeal printed in the *Gospel Trumpet* from a man by the name of Isaac DeLevante. He had come across a copy of this paper and was delighted with the message it contained and so he wrote asking that someone come to Jamaica to preach. The Olsons labored faithfully on the island for forty-six years and others served for shorter periods. By 1975 there were eighty-nine congregations of the Church of God in Jamaica and the work was largely indigenous. The church operates Ardenne High School in Kingston with a student body of 800. Jamaica School of Theology functions as a training center for expanding leadership needs.

Through the efforts of many other missionaries the work of the Church of God later spread to the Cayman Islands, to Cuba, and to Puerto Rico. In 1967 the Missionary Board joined with the missions board of the National Association of the Church of God in maintaining work on the islands of Antigua, St. Kitts, and Curacao.

Egypt

Once the interest in expansion to foreign lands was aroused, there was no stopping it. The leaders began traveling abroad, and everywhere they went they saw opportunities. G. P. Tasker and H. A. Brooks, for instance, were on their way to India in 1907 to assist in the missionary work there. They stopped in Egypt for a short time and were impressed with its possibilities as a field for evangelization. They wrote back to America suggesting that someone go to Egypt. By November of that same year E. A. Reardon was there. He spent most of his time for the next year at Assiut on the Upper Nile and was able to spend a short time at Alexandria. When Reardon returned to America in 1908 he left the work under the leadership of G. K. Ouzounian, an Armenian minister whom he had been able to lead out of the Adventist church. With the exception of short periods of evangelistic work by the F. G. Smiths in 1913 and the H. M. Riggles in 1921, Ouzounian carried the great burden of the work until after the arrival of the Thaddeus Neffs in 1923 as missionaries from the United States.

The Neffs spent the remaining twenty-eight years of their ministry in Egypt. In the 1940s they were joined by the Wilbur Skaggs. Later there were many others who served the cause of mission outreach in Egypt, including the Kenneth Croses, the Lester Croses, the Jean Kilmers, the William Fleenors, and the James Simpsons. The last resident missionaries there were the Ernest LaFonts who left Cairo in 1971, leaving the churches in the hands of national leaders. The LaFonts did return to the eastern Mediteranean area, however, and established residence in Beruit in order to be geographically available for assistance to churches in Lebanon, Greece, and Italy, as well as Egypt. The Egyptian churches are relatively small and lack adequate leadership, but they operate two youth centers in Cairo and Alexandria and cooperate with three other Christian groups in sponsoring the Nile Christian Bookshops as a vehicle for literature distribution.

Japan

The work of the Church of God reformation was extended to Japan in 1908. The man responsible for its beginning was Ukichi Yajima. Yajima had been converted at the age of nineteen and in 1900 was ordained as a Presbyterian minister. He served churches in Tokyo and in the Hawaiian Islands. He was not satisfied with his Christian experience, however, so he came to California in 1905 hoping to find a deeper knowledge of Christ by fellowship with American Christians. It was here that he came in contact with the Church of God.

Late one night Yajima was riding an interurban train from Oakland to San Francisco. A lady in the front of the car got off and left a paper on the seat. He picked it up and began to read. It was a copy of the *Gospel Trumpet.* He was especially interested in an article on divine healing, and so he wrote to the editor. E. E. Byrum directed him to contact some of the brethren in California, which he did. Yajima found the kind of Christianity he had been seeking. After spending some time in creating interest in Japanese missions among the churches in America he returned to Japan in 1908 and began to work among his own people. The next year he was joined by three missionaries from the United States, J. D. Hatch and Mr. and Mrs. W. G. Alexander. Other workers followed, including the Adam W. Millers and Axchie Bolitho. Most of the work was centered in and around the city of Tokyo.

By World War II six congregations and a Bible institute had been established. During the fighting, however, all the missionaries were withdrawn, the Christians were scattered, and all but one of the church buildings were destroyed by bombs or fire. Following the peace treaty the church in the United States began to furnish aid and by 1950 to once again send missionaries. The first couple to go was the Arthur Eikamps. During the next twenty-five years they were joined by the Nathan Smiths, the Donald Goens, the Philip Kinleys, Freda LaFoe, the Orlo Kretlows, Karen Evans, Patricia Bentley, and the Ronald Mauers. By 1975 the church in Japan had developed nine congregations, a high school for girls, a "Seminary House" to supplement training for leaders, and a number of weekday kindergartens. A missionary extension of this mission church has been the establishment of a new work in Okinawa.

China

Contact with China was first made through two brothers, William A. and Charles E. Hunnex. Both had been born in

China, the sons of English missionaries. In 1904 both of them came to America. Here they heard the message of the Church of God reformation and accepted the truth which was proclaimed. After working for a while in the Gospel Trumpet office and in the missionary homes in Chicago and New York they began to think of going back to China. In 1909 William Hunnex and his wife, Gloria, went to Chinkiang and opened a mission station. The next year Charles Hunnex and Pina Winters joined them. Within four years there were four stations with six Chinese pastors in addition to the missionaries.

Other workers were added in 1915 when Daisy V. Maiden and Belle M. Watson went to China. In 1923 Mr. and Mrs. Karl M. Kreutz joined the corps of workers in that country. Several new stations were opened. In 1927, however, the Chinese Civil War forced all of the missionaries to flee to Shanghai and later to other parts of the world. The Kreutzes went to the Philippines and carried on mission work there for a number of years.

During the 1940s it was possible to reopen several of the mission stations in China and to develop plans for the building of a hospital. To implement these dreams a number of additional missionaries were sent, including the Dr. David Gaulkes, Lovena Billings, the Milton Buettners, and the Edgar Williams. By 1947 the Communist invasion forced all of these either to come home or to move to West China which was unoccupied by the Communists at that time. Two years later, however, there was complete evacuation of all missionaries.

There are, however, two continuing centers of outreach by the Church of God in East Asia—one in Hong Kong and the other in the Philippines. The Haven of Hope Sanitorium is under the direction of Dr. Peter Jenkins whose wife is the former Lovena Billings. The Church of God became affiliated with this already-operating medical facility in 1969 as a cooperating sponsor. In the Philippines the reopening of the work came about through the ministry of Roland Bacani, a Filipino who studied at Gulf-Coast Bible College and returned to start a congregation and school in Manila.

Lebanon

The work of the Church of God in Lebanon dates back to the year 1912. It was another instance of visitors sending a call for help. Mrs. George P. Tasker and Bessie Hittle (later Mrs. R. R. Byrum) had secured positions to teach for a term in a native village school at Schweifat near Beirut. Almost from the moment of arrival they began to write back to America that opportunities for missionary work were unlimited. When Mrs. Tasker's husband came by to pick her up on the way to India later that same year he brought with him a very capable missionary team, F. G. and Birdie Smith and their son Gerald. Mrs. Tasker's teaching position was taken by Nellie Laughlin of Vermont. When the Smiths and Bessie Hittle returned to America in 1914, Miss Laughlin gave up her teaching and became a full-time missionary. Then came World War I, and all contact with Miss Laughlin was cut off. Through the help of friends she was able to carry on through those difficult years. In 1921 she was joined by H. M. and Minnie Riggle who stayed for two years. Later the John D. Croses arrived and served there until 1949. Since 1950 the work of the church in Lebanon has been carried on entirely by national leaders. In addition to several congregations they have developed a camp, an orphanage, and a youth center near the American University.

East Africa

The mission stations operated by the Church of God in Kenya were established early in the twentieth century by A. W. Baker, of the South African Compounds Mission. Baker's daughter, Mabel, and Mr. and Mrs. H. C. Kramer were put in charge of this outpost.

In 1921 Baker found it difficult to finance this station in addition to his South African work so he instructed Kramer to make contact with some evangelical group which might be interested in taking over this work. Through literature from the Gospel Trumpet Company which Kramer had been reading since 1912 he was already acquainted with the Church of God movement, and so he came to America and presented the matter to the Missionary Board in Anderson. The opportunity seemed challenging, and arrangements were made to assume responsibility for operating this mission. When the Kramers returned in 1922 they were missionaries of the Church of God.

Other workers quickly followed, and through the succeeding years an increasing number was sent to staff the expanding program. In some years as many as forty missionaries have been deployed to this field. It is not possible here to name all who have served in this African mission enterprise, but a few outstanding long-term leaders should be noted. In addition to Mabel Baker, particular mention should be made of the John S. Ludwigs, Jewell Hall, Lima Lehmer, the Reuben Schweigers, the Frank LaFonts, Lydia Hansen, and Irene Engst, all of whom spent twenty years or more as missionaries in Africa.

East Africa was to become the largest of all the outposts of the Church of God outside the United States, comprising, by the mid 1970s, about 35,000 adult Christians in 350 congregations. The earliest and largest center of witness is at Kima. The central administrative offices of all the work in East Africa are located here, as well as Kima Theological College, a hospital, and two high schools. Other centers are located at Mwihila, Ingotse, Shitoli, and Ibeno. A major extension of the 1960s and 1970s was toward the rapidly developing urban areas. Work was established in ten of the larger cities, with the greatest attention being given to the capital city of Nairobi where eight congregations were developed. In 1959 the work was extended to Tanzania. Mission centers were developed in three areas—Kaiti, Mbulu, and Mirambo. Still later, through the efforts of Kenya Christians, the work of the Church of God was planted in the neighboring nation of Uganda and at least six congregations were established.

Along with evangelization the mission extended its services in applying the Christian witness to other aspects of the life of the people, particularly education and health. At least eighty primary schools and four high schools were established. After

Kenya's independence all these became government operated, but the religious training curriculum is developed by church leaders. Two hospitals and several outpatient clinics and medical dispensaries are in operation at the various mission stations.

Beginning around 1948 the African church moved toward self-governance. In that year the first delegated General Assembly was organized and in 1961 it elected its first African chairman. In 1972 the Missionary Board turned over the titles of all properties to the Church of God in East Africa. Since that time the administrative leadership is all African and, although missionaries from America still serve, they are sent only as requested by the African assembly.

Central America

The church is at work in three Central American countries—Panama, Costa Rica, and Guatemala. In each of these places churches began by local initiative before any missionaries were sent. The first development was in Panama in 1910. By the 1970s there were twenty congregations, nine of which were on the San Blas Islands among the Cuna Tribe. Since 1959 the Dean Floras have guided national leaders in developments in that area. In Costa Rica the church began through the witness of Christians from Jamaica. There are four congregations with the major thrust during the 1970s being directed toward strengthening the work in the capital city of San Jose. In Guatemala the church was started by a Costa Rican minister in the late 1960s. Ten congregations developed, all of which function under national leadership.

South America

By 1975 there were congregations of the Church of God in eight countries of South America. The earliest contact on this continent was in Guyana in 1914 when G. L. Jeffrey, the leader of a group of independent Christians there, learned of the movement and identified with it through contact with some

Trinidad missionaries who went to the mainland to hold meetings. Later a succession of missionaries was sent to assist in the work. In 1971 the churches there began functioning under their own leadership.

In southern Brazil and northern Argentina the church was started and developed by immigrants from Germany who went there as early as 1923 and took their message with them. For almost a half century their ministry was carried on in the German language and mostly among other German immigrants, but in the early 1970s many of the more than fifty congregations changed to the national languages of Portuguese and Spanish and their work was extended across the Argentina border into Paraguay. Through assistance from the missionary board in North America a training school, Boa Terra, was started in 1972 in Curitiba, Brazil with Maurice and Dondeena Caldwell as the initiators. The following year the Brazilian church and the North American church developed a cooperative strategy for extending the work in northern Brazil in the area of Itaituba along the new trans-Amazon highway.

In 1958 the Paul Butzes went to Peru, on their own initiative, and found opportunity for Christian witness in the jungle area of Pucallpa. In 1971 they were appointed as missionaries. Several congregations and a training school have developed. A new congregation was launched in the capital city of Lima. To the north in Venezuela a cooperative work with the Churches of God in North America was established in 1975. In the same year the Homer Firestones, long-time missionaries in Bolivia, identified with the Church of God and brought with them a ministry to approximately 8,000 persons among the Quechua and Aimaru Indians. A year earlier a similar contact with a small evangelical mission in Uruguay brought a congregation of about one hundred people into fellowship with the movement.

Korea, Australia, Guam

The extension of the Church of God into Korea came about in 1937 when an already existing Christian group affiliated with the movement. No missionaries were sent until 1955 when the John Croses were in South Korea for a year. In 1962 the Kenneth Goods began a five-year term to give assistance in starting a Bible school. Since 1967 the church there has functioned independently with only occasional contact with American leaders.

In Australia the work began around 1917 when E. P. May returned to his native country with the message of the Church of God. Progress was slow but the church was persistent. Beginning in 1954 a succession of ministers from America and West Germany moved to Australia to assist in evangelism and in the development of new congregations and a Bible school, bringing a great deal of new life and enthusiasm to the work there.

On the island of Guam a Church of God congregation developed among American service personnel stationed there following World War II. Its outreach extended to Filipinos and native Guamanians. Leaders include William E. Rife and Filipe Merioles who have led the group in securing land and building a chapel.

An Ongoing Process

By 1975 the Church of God was functioning in fifty-three countries of the world. It has not been possible to detail all the developments in this brief review. Sufficient has been said, however, to indicate that the Church of God reformation embraces a worldwide fellowship. Those who have felt the burden to go out have been prompted by the same motives that have always impelled sincere Christians to witness in the far corners of the world. They have responded to Christ's command to "go make disciples of all nations." In these developing areas the message of the unity of all true believers has been especially pertinent, for here more than anywhere else sectarianism is a tragic evil. The passing of the years has brought an ever-expanding vision of the possibilities of "one great fellowship of love throughout the whole wide earth."

Points for Discussion

1. Why was the Church of God more than ten years old before there was much interest in foreign missions?

2. By what means did leaders become interested in carrying the message to foreign lands?

3. Give a brief sketch of how the Church of God work was started in Canada, in Europe, in India, in China, in Africa, in South America.

4. What have been the main motives in the extension of the Church of God to foreign lands?

5. Should the Church of God compete with other Christian groups in missionary work in non-Christian lands? Explain.

CHAPTER VI

CONSOLIDATING GAINS

The feverish pace set by the "flying ministry" in the early years of the Church of God reformation established the general pattern of activity until well into the twentieth century. Evangelists continued to be ever on the move, going to and fro, proclaiming the message God had given them. Their strenuous schedules could hardly be duplicated today, even with all the improvements in transportation and communication. Warner, for instance, tells of going for weeks without missing a day in preaching from one to four times. It was not uncommon for him to spend as many as eight hours in the pulpit in one day besides the time spent with people at the altar. Accounts of the activities of other evangelists such as H. M. Riggle, W. G. Schell, and F. G. Smith tell a similar story. Theirs was certainly a life dominated by a burning passion.

By the early 1890s, however, certain tendencies were beginning to develop which would change this pattern somewhat. In the March 10, 1892, issue of the *Gospel Trumpet*, for example, an editorial warns congregations against building houses for preachers. "Beware," Warner says, "how you through selfish motives of having frequent preaching lay a snare to entangle God's flying messengers. . . . This is the time of the end, and God's messengers must run to and fro." He continues with some advice to the preachers themselves, telling them to avoid becoming attached to worldly things that would keep them from going where the Lord directed. If they had real need of a house it was better to buy rather than take the time to build. Besides, it was cheaper. That such an article was written is pretty good evidence that several congregations were feeling the need of a settled pastor, and that some of the "flying messengers" were beginning to be inclined to fold their wings and settle down in a nest for a season.

This editorial, urging the flying ministry to keep on flying, is tempered somewhat by another which appeared the following week entitled, "Leave Not Too Soon." It had come to the editor's attention that some of the messengers were "flying" too fast. He cites instances in which a good meeting would be reported at a given place and then a year later another evangelist would go to this same place and find no fruits remaining. Foundations for the truth would have to be laid all over again. "Now, beloved," says Warner, "this is a great waste of time. Why blow the bellows and heat the iron, and then throw it out to cool. . . . Dear brethren, see to it that your labor is not largely lost by quitting too soon." This was at least the beginning of a justification for resident pastors.

In the main, however, these tendencies did not prevail for almost another quarter century. The extension of concern to foreign lands kept the pioneer spirit vigorously alive and counterbalanced any overt tendencies toward settling down at home.

Time Was Running Out

The chief motivation for this rapid ministry was, of course, the belief that the end of time was very near. In the earliest period a general conviction prevailed that the return of the Lord could be expected momentarily. It was important that at least a few be snatched from the clutches of Satan before it was too late. In prophetic words the ministers declared that the clouds of division and strife which had obscured the light of truth at midday were now breaking up and passing away. The light was breaking through, but it was the "evening time." The evening light was now shining brightly, but night was near. The work had to be done while it was yet day, "for the night cometh when no man can work."

Warner is said to have stated on several occasions that he expected the end to come during his own lifetime. No written statement of this has been found, but from the tenor of some of his writings, such as the song entitled "The Lord Is Near at

Hand," there is little doubt that this expectation was very real to him. By 1895, the year of his death, however, Warner had apparently modified his anticipation somewhat. In an editorial in the *Gospel Trumpet* (January 3, 1895) he writes:

> We know it is the last time. . . . And yet, beloved, we deem it safe to say to you all what we have only mentioned to a few individuals, and that is our conviction by the word of God that perhaps as much as forty years more may elapse ere the Judge of all shall proclaim the end of time and the doom of all men.

This modification was to exert a great influence on the pattern of development in the movement. An extension of time even up to forty years gave good reason to begin structuring the work on a more permanent basis. At least a rudimentary organization, the acquisition of property, and a limited amount of planning ahead could be justified on the grounds of insuring that those who had seen the light should remain faithful, if for no other reasons. The full implications of this modification were to be seen in the developments which took place in the closing years of the nineteenth century and the first three decades of the twentieth.

Development of Congregations

From the very beginning of the reformation activity those who accepted the truth in each locality met together for fellowship and devotion. It was inevitable that these worshiping units should eventually develop some kind of organization. As the number of "saints" in various places increased they found it impossible to continue to meet in their homes. Where schoolhouses or other public buildings were available these were often procured as meeting places. In many situations, however, no such arrangements could be made, and so it became necessary either to rent a meeting place or to buy or build one. In either case, some organization was required. Someone had to be designated to handle funds and, if property were bought, some arrangements had to be made for the group to hold title to it.

On the surface these appear to be relatively simple matters, but to the early reformers these details posed some rather difficult theological problems. They felt that sect organization was unscriptural. From the beginning they had preached against all "man rule." How to select a congregational officer, such as a treasurer, or name a board of trustees to hold property without violating the principles they maintained was a matter of some concern.

The problem had apparently become sufficiently general by 1893 to prompt the editor of the *Gospel Trumpet* to give some guidance to congregations wrestling with this matter. In the November 23 issue he mentions that some readers had asked how to obtain a deed to a meeting house and still avoid any unscriptural action. In answering, Warner first notes that the specific legal requirements for the corporate holding of property in each state must be checked before proceedings are begun. Then, in a meeting of the congregation "a minister or any brother" may suggest the names of those who would be considered elders or deacons (the only officers authorized in the New Testament). These and their successors could be considered the trustees. In order to meet the legal requirement of election of trustees, the congregation could cast their vote for these people by saying amen. This would avoid voting by ballot, which was considered "contrary to the principles of the body of Christ." Such a process also made it unnecessary to do any more voting later since the appointed elders would always be the successors of the original trustees.

This suggested procedure, while not representative of the practice in most modern congregations, indicates quite clearly that organization of local congregations was sanctioned at a very early date. In the course of the next few years more and more churches secured their own property. Exact figures for the earlier period are not available, but by 1919 the statistics published in the *Yearbook* indicate that 450 of the 1,097 congregations owned their own places of worship. Another significant development is indicated in the notation that 925 of these congregations had resident pastors. This was an almost complete reversal of the situation thirty years earlier.

The Publishing Work

The oldest structured general agency connected with the Church of God reformation is, of course, the publishing work. The Gospel Trumpet Company was, in fact, older than the movement itself, so there was no organizational problem as far as the reformers were concerned as to how a printing establishment would be started. They simply accepted this enterprise as an important part of their ministry. Since the company was privately rather than corporately owned for the first twenty years or so, the issue of ecclesiastical control was not raised during the early period.

The first pattern of business organization was that of a partnership, with Warner holding at least a one-third interest during his lifetime. The first partner was Haines who withdrew within a short time. Next came J. C. Fisher. Other partners at various times included D. D. Johnson, W. G. Schell, Sebastian Michels, E. E. Byrum, and N. H. Byrum.

Partnership in this instance did not involve receiving a share of the profits, for there were none. It simply was a means of designating who would get what in case the company dissolved and the assets were distributed. No one who invested in the company ever received either interest or dividends. Furthermore, those who worked in the Trumpet Office for the first thirty-five years received no wages or salaries. Their food, lodging, and clothing were furnished, and in later years they were given a dollar a week for spending money. Whatever surplus there might have been was used to buy new equipment or to send out free literature.

Shortly after the time of Warner's death some agitation arose to put the company under the control of a wider cross section of the brethren. Accordingly, under the direction of Arthur S. Potter, of Omaha, Nebraska, plans for a stock company were drawn up and put in effect after the company had moved to

Moundsville, West Virginia, in 1898. The shares sold at one dollar each to people in the Church of God, were noninterest-bearing, and could not be recalled for a period of five years. Provision was made for electing trustees, a board of directors, and officers for the company. Though the base of control was enlarged it still remained, from a legal standpoint, a private corporation.

As the work expanded it became expedient to reincorporate as a nonprofit organization. Accordingly, in 1903 all the stock was recalled and a new corporation was formed. When the move was made to Anderson, Indiana, in 1906, this same type of structure was established under Indiana laws governing organizations set up not for profit. This arrangement proved much more satisfactory, but still there was no direct control by the church as a whole since the eleven members of the company named their own successors within the limits prescribed in the bylaws. In 1917, however, the number of members was increased to twenty-four and all were to be elected by the General Ministerial Assembly. This put the company directly under the control of the church as represented by the body of ministers meeting annually in Anderson, Indiana. This structure has been modified only slightly in the years since that time. The most significant changes came in 1962 when the legal name of the company was changed to Warner Press, Incorporated, and in 1972 when the elected governing board for the company, designated as the Publication Board of the Church of God, was increased in size from twenty-four to twenty-five members.

The Missionary Enterprise

The story of the expansion of the Church of God reformation to many foreign countries has already been told. In reviewing these accounts of how the work began in various continents it will be noted that the Missionary Board is hardly mentioned. The reason is that most of these contacts were made, and the mission work was well under way, before a Missionary Board was ever created. The early missionaries went out without any responsible backing whatever. Their only means of support consisted of personal contributions made by friends and others who responded to appeals made in the letter column of the *Gospel Trumpet*. As might be expected, these responses were spasmodic and irregular and gave the missionaries little assurance of continued support in their work.

The first attempt at giving any structure to the missionary work came in October of 1898 when a special account, "the Missionary Fund," was established by the Gospel Trumpet Company for receiving money sent in for work abroad. All who wished to contribute toward the support of missionaries already on the field and to provide means for sending more workers could do so through this channel.

By 1909, however, the extent of missionary activity had increased so greatly, and the problems arising in connection with the foreign work were of such magnitude, that a more adequate structure was imperative. In addition to the financial problem, a multitude of decisions had to be made as to who should go where and when. When the ministers met during the Anderson Camp Meeting that year they were asked to approve the appointment of seven brethren to act as a missionary committee. Structurally, this committee was related to the only other agency then in existence, the Gospel Trumpet Company. The duties of this committee consisted of "advising, instructing, encouraging, or restraining those who feel called to the foreign missionary field" and collecting and disbursing the missionary funds of the church. In 1917 this committee became officially the Missionary Board of the Church of God, incorporated under the laws of Indiana, and responsible to the General Ministerial Assembly. The number of members was increased to eleven at this time and later, in 1921, to fifteen.

The General Assembly

From the beginning the reformers had held what they called "assemblies." These were gatherings in the winter similar to the camp meetings in the summer and were designed to bring together all the "saints" within a particular area. Later some of these meetings were called for ministers only, so they were labeled "ministerial assemblies." Still later it became common practice to have special sessions for ministers during the camp meetings. These meetings gave the ministers opportunity to discuss their problems and to exhort each other in regard to upholding the doctrines.

The meeting of ministers during the annual camp meeting at Anderson, Indiana, came to be the largest and most significant of these ministerial assemblies. When the growth of the work demanded some central agency to which all the other developing aspects of the work could be tied, this assembly seemed to be the logical place for the structure to be focused. Consequently, in June of 1917 the General Ministerial Assembly was organized and designated as the body responsible for controlling the various agencies of the church. The two agencies then in existence, the Gospel Trumpet Company and the Missionary Board, were immediately placed under the Assembly's jurisdiction. Other general agencies which have been created as needs have arisen have been placed within this same basic framework. By 1921 the Missionary Board found its overseas operations so demanding that it was relieved of its responsibilities for home missions, and a new agency, the Board of Church Extension and Home Missions, was created. In 1923 the growing concern for promoting and improving educational activity in local churches led to the formation of the Board of Religious Education and Sunday Schools (later designated as the Board of Christian Education). In 1925 the Bible Training School which had been operating as the educational department of Gospel Trumpet Company was given autonomous status and related to the General Ministerial Assembly as Anderson Bible School and Seminary (later renamed Anderson College). In 1949 a pension program for ministers and church workers was launched and its operation was placed under a newly created Board of Pensions functioning under the Assembly. Then two more of the church's colleges were elevated to the status of general agencies and made subject to the Assembly, Pacific Bible College (later, Warner Pacific College) in 1949, and Gulf-Coast Bible College in 1968.

Membership on these general boards was not limited to ministers and, in the course of the years, several lay people were elected to these positions by the General Ministerial Assembly. In order to include these lay people more fully in the decision making processes, provision was made to open the Assembly to them. Accordingly, in 1965 the name of the governing body itself was changed by dropping the word *ministerial* from its title, making it simply The General Assembly of the Church of God.

The Executive Council

In order to provide for administrative and legal functions relating to the General Assembly and to coordinate the varied work of the eight general agencies it became expedient for the Assembly to create a comprehensively based structure which could perform these duties for the Assembly when it was not in session. Accordingly, in 1932 the Assembly authorized the organization of an Executive Council. Then in 1954 and 1957, after extensive study by a special commission, the scope of the Council's responsibilities was expanded to encompass the operation of three divisions: World Service, Church Service, and General Service. Likewise, certain commissions authorized by the Assembly were to function under the Executive Council: the Radio and Television Commission, the Commission on Christian Higher Education, and the Commission on Social Concerns. The Executive Council functioned without a full-time executive until the late 1950s when Clarence W. Hatch was named the first executive secretary. Following his death in 1960 Charles V. Weber filled the position for eleven years until his retirement. In 1971 W. E. Reed assumed responsibilities for this central office for the national work of the Church of God.

Organization at the national level was followed by development of cooperative structures by the clusters of congregations in states and provinces. Area assemblies had been held from the earliest period of the movement's history, but these had been meetings primarily for inspiration and fellowship. By the 1920s some of these assemblies were conducting certain corporate business functions such as planning general meetings and managing properties where camp meetings were held. In 1925 Elver F. Adcock, registrar for the national *Yearbook,* asked sectional "registration committees" to approve the names of persons from their area to be listed in that annual publication. Regional authority was further enhanced in 1930 when Charles E. Brown, the editor of the *Gospel Trumpet,* placed the responsibility on state and provincial committees to approve persons whose articles and field reports would be eligible for inclusion in the church magazine. During the following decades the number of these regional organizations continued to increase and their functions to expand. Most have formed their own boards and committees parallel to and cooperative with those in the national structure. By 1975 there were fourteen states or regions whose programs had developed to the point of employing full-time staff persons to direct and coordinate their corporate activities.

The Basic Principle

A rapid survey, such as this has been, of the organizational developments in the Church of God reformation might seem to indicate a great departure from the basic concepts of the pioneers in regard to church government. A closer look at their real beliefs, however, reveals that the departure has not been so drastic as it might at first appear.

The early reformers were opposed to organization because they saw that the Holy Spirit was given little opportunity to direct in the ecclesiastical systems then in operation. They abhorred all man-made organization, for they could see how it tended to become rigid and inflexible and to interfere with the free operation of the Spirit. Furthermore, an ecclesiastical system based on elected officials seemed to be inconsistent with the true nature of the church in which the Lord was supposed to "set the members in the body as it pleases him." The evil to which they were really opposed, then, was human interference with God's plan.

As the work grew, the necessity of making certain persons or groups responsible for particular aspects of the work became obviously imperative. But how could these people be named to their responsibility without some kind of organization? A possible answer was suggested along about 1919 when the idea of "charismatic" government was introduced. It was asserted that the Holy Spirit designated people to the various offices, and others were to recognize each person's "gift" and acknowledge his right to his office. This was generally acknowledged as a proper ideal to maintain. From a practical standpoint, however, there was always the question of what would happen should there not be general recognition of a person's gift, or if more than one person claimed divine leadings to the same office.

After many years of struggling with this problem it eventually came to be held that the Holy Spirit was not limited to one method of revealing himself; he could work through a committee or a congregation as well as an individual. Furthermore, he could direct people in their voting as well as in their actions. This is in full keeping with God's basic method of operation, which is the using of people to accomplish his will. It is also consistent with the teaching of the pioneers, for it does not constitute "man rule" but rather God rule through consecrated men.

Points for Discussion

1. Must a reformation go through a "cooling-off" period?
2. Trace the development of the organization of local congregations in the Church of God.
3. What was the role of the Gospel Trumpet Company in the development of the national agencies?
4. How would the history of the movement have been different if the necessary organization had been developed before the need became acute?

5. Are present tendencies inconsistent with the principles set forth by the pioneers? Explain.

CHAPTER VII

THE MINISTRY OF TEACHING

In a movement in which the primary emphasis was on a "flying messenger" preaching type of evangelism it would hardly be expected that a great deal of attention would be given to teaching as a method of reaching and winning people to the cause. In the main, this was the case. Teaching is a long-range process, and the results are less immediate. The pioneers were interested in accomplishing as much as possible in the shortest time. In addition, there was a pretty general suspicion of anything that went under the label of education—a term associated with such carnal attitudes as pride and self-sufficiency. A particular odium attached to ministers who depended on their seminary training rather than on the Lord for their knowledge and inspiration.

Under these conditions it is somewhat surprising to discover rather early indications that at least some attention was given to the teaching ministry. Despite the tendency to reject all that was associated with the sects, there seems to have been no general rejection of Sunday schools on that ground. A definite statement to this effect comes from the pen of Warner as early as 1885. A reader asks specifically if Sabbath schools are scriptural and if it is right to conduct them. Warner replies at length in the December 1 issue of the *Gospel Trumpet:*

> Concerning Sabbath schools, we answer that we read of no such thing in the Word of God. The Sabbath schools, as ordinarily conducted in Babylon, are schools of vanity, and hotbeds of pride and false religion. Let all saints keep themselves and children out of all such fashionable, worldly gatherings. Have no fellowship with them.
>
> Yet to properly teach our children the fear of God, the love of Christ, and the way of virtue and salvation is one of the most important duties upon parents, and one too that is greatly neglected. . . .

Most of the religious training should be given to children at home. Yet where there are a sufficient number of saints to hold a service especially for the instruction of the children and youths, there is no reason why such service should not be held. But it must not be after the popular style. It must be held in the Spirit of Christ, all the teachers being holy. It must not have the fashionable corps of officers, or any of that sort, but let it be a part of the regular worship of God. Let the Elders and others apt to teach, instruct, and the Holy Spirit preside instead of a voted in superintendent.

Two year later (September 1, 1887) Allie R. Fisher wrote an article, with an endorsement note by Warner, entitled, "Teach Your Children the Lord." This article was quite obviously designed to break down the prejudice against Sunday schools which apparently existed in the minds of some. The writer presents a strong defense of Sunday schools as a means of "cultivating the minds of the children to receive the truth." At the same time there is no compromise at the point of using anything but the Bible for the curriculum. "We have no use for lesson leaves," she says, ". . . but take the Word of God and let them read it." There is, however, a suggestion that the children "be graded into classes of different ages, so there will be no time lost, nor any neglected."

Encouragement and Guidance

The years that followed certainly saw no great all-out effort to promote Sunday schools, but neither were the leaders disposed to denounce them entirely. Most of the early articles in the *Gospel Trumpet* dealing with the subject are careful to point out, as did Warner in the statement quoted, that these schools are not to be the same type as those existing in the sectarian churches. Sunday schools continued and actually became a means of conserving the work of the "flying ministry." In many places those who had "come out" as the result of a revival campaign held their group together after the evangelist was gone by organizing a Sunday school.

By the later 1880s an educational technique had even invaded the revival campaigns. Many of the evangelists, including Warner, began conducting children's meetings along with their evangelistic services. F. G. Smith tells how he was converted in 1890 in one of these meetings on the Bangor, Michigan, campground. The women members of the evangelistic companies often made these meetings a regular part of their ministry. A number of songs were composed and printed especially for use with children. One of the lyrics appearing in 1891 went like this:

There is something for children to do,
In the vineyard of Jesus today;
They can speak gentle words as they go;
They can preach little sermons and pray.

It needs to be recognized, of course, that the object of these meetings was primarily to help children make a definite commitment of their lives to Christ, but the fact remains that the method employed was that of the classroom rather than the pulpit.

One of the clearest descriptions of the standard set for Sunday schools during this early period is found in an article by E. E. Byrum entitled, "Sunday School Work," appearing in the June 1, 1889, *Gospel Trumpet.* After observing that "this great work of the Lord has been sadly neglected," he then launches into a rather lengthy defense of such a program of instruction. This is followed by suggestions as to how to conduct a Sunday school. Some of the principles set forth are still quite pertinent:

> See to it that each class is supplied with a holy teacher who is capable of giving the proper instruction. The classes should not be too large, and should be arranged according to the age and natural ability. . . . In no case should arguing be allowed. . . . Good singing is one of the necessary things to give spiritual life to the work. . . . The study for the Bible classes should be kept up during the week, as well as on Sabbath. . . . It is not good to offer general prizes, as it gives place for strife and division. . . . May the Lord stir up the hearts of the people to a sense of duty in regard to this work.

Helps for Teachers

The establishment of Sunday schools and the holding of children's meetings soon created a demand for especially designed materials. The first attempt at producing literature for children came, not from the Gospel Trumpet Company, but from the private press of C. L. Kaumeyer of Chippewa, Ontario, in 1889. The proposed name for this publication was Evening Light for the Children. When the first issue appeared, however, it was called the *Guide.* For some reason this paper failed to find an audience. Perhaps the need for such a publication was not yet generally felt, or, more probably, promotion was insufficient. At any rate, Kaumeyer was forced to discontinue the paper after only a few issues.

About eighteen months later, in January of 1891, publication of a children's paper by the Gospel Trumpet Office was begun. The *Shining Light* was a four-page monthly, "devoted to the interests of children; yet, we expect older ones to be interested in reading the same." The editor, E. E. Byrum, stated, "The language will be simple and easily understood, and we shall deal with facts instead of fiction." This was the first regularly issued piece of curriculum material produced by the Church of God reformation. The popularity of this paper was almost immediate. Within a year it is reported that over one hundred thousand copies had been published. A decade later one of the main features was a regular "Bible Lesson" which was obviously designed to be used in classes. By 1907 the material in the paper had come to be designed for older children and young people to such an extent that the publishers decided to produce "another small paper calculated to interest and instruct the little ones, who are yet too young to comprehend the Bible lessons and stories printed in the *Shining Light.*" The first issue of *Our Little Folks* appeared in June of 1907.

Three years later, in 1910, the first regular Sunday school quarterlies were published by the Gospel Trumpet Company. These were to contain the main portion of the lesson presentations, and the story papers were to be used as supplementary material. The quarterlies were based on the International Uniform Lesson Series, and suggestions were made for adapting them to four age levels—primary, junior, intermediate, and senior. It was not until around 1926 that specifically graded materials were issued, and these also were based on the Uniform Series. In another nine years, however, a senior youth quarterly based on a life-centered curriculum was launched. The success of this venture quickly led to an extension of graded materials to all other departments on the children and youth levels.

The most ambitious project in the development of teaching materials came in 1969 when Warner Press and the Board of Christian Education joined with leaders from three other church groups in producing an entirely new Sunday morning curriculum for all age groups. Under the designation, "Ventures in Christian Living," a biblically based and educationally sound cycle of quarterly materials was carefully planned, expertly written, and introduced to the church. Of particular significance, from the standpoint of both instruction and promotion, was the method of presentation which involved the setting up of regional convocations in 151 locations in the United States and Canada at which informed leaders trained almost 13,000 persons who would be using the new materials. The whole curriculum was supported by a series of study books for leaders and adult classes dealing with the foundational themes and perspectives of the age-group materials themselves.

In addition to Sunday morning lessons the educational agencies of the church also have either produced or made available study and program materials for vacation church schools, youth meetings, day camps, nursery schools, day-care centers, and other learning ventures related to the educational ministry of the church.

Organization for Education

It has already been noted that though Sunday schools were accepted in the earliest period a strong aversion was felt toward organizing them. In many instances there was little or no organization, and various people performed the various functions as they were "led of the Spirit" to do so. Even under such a loose system as this, however, usually someone was regarded as being "in charge." By the late 1880s there seems to have been a realization that if education was to be effective it must have specific people assigned to the various responsibilites. This was the pattern followed when the first Sunday school was organized by the Trumpet Family in Grand Junction, Michigan. An entry in the diary of G. J. Detweiler, one of the workers, for July 24, 1892, reads:

> Those who are left at home all walked to the Tabernacle. Bro. A.L.B. [A. L. Byers] preached in the forenoon. Sunday school begun in the afternoon with E.E.B. [E. E. Byrum] Supt. and Andrew [Byers] & Belle [Isabel Costen], I, and Bro. Wooden take the classes. Lesson Mat. 2 and Mat. 1 & others for ref. Text Mat. 1:21.

Later entries indicate how the classes were divided and tell of other passages which were used for study. When Byrum was absent someone else was named to act in his place as superintendent.

Development of Sunday school work for the next several years was apparently steady but quite slow, with very little guidance being given to those who were engaged in this work. The advent of the Uniform Lesson quarterlies in 1910, however, added impetus to the organization of Sunday schools, and the demands for help eventually brought some leaders to the fore who could give the needed assistance. The most notable of these was D. O. Teasley. In company with A. D. Khan from India, who was visiting in America at that time, Teasley visited many churches and taught leaders how to organize and administer their Sunday schools.

In 1911 Teasley wrote a book, *How to Conduct a Sunday School,* in which he makes it clear that the organization of the Sunday school is not the organization of the church. "The church is a divine organization," he writes, "and its membership is composed only of those who have salvation. The

Sunday school, on the contrary, is a human organization for a divine purpose, and its membership includes all who wish to know the truth." He outlines the organization of the Sunday school, describes the responsibilities of the various officers, suggests regular teachers' meetings, tells how to prepare and teach a lesson, and deals with a variety of problems which face those responsible for the educational program of the church. This was, by far, the most progressive step taken in Sunday school work up to that time.

A National Program

It was to be another dozen years, though, before there was sufficient interest in the work of Christian education to create a national agency for the promotion and guidance of this activity. In 1923 a resolution introduced in the General Ministerial Assembly provided for the creation of a Board of Religious Education and Sunday Schools. This resolution was adopted and the first Board was elected. R. L. Berry was the first president.

For the first several years the work of the Board was mainly in two areas: (1) promotion of teacher training, and (2) establishing standards and goals for effective programs of Christian education. In this early period the work was mostly in providing course outlines and recommending materials. The earliest executives of the new board were volunteer leaders who were employed elsewhere but had deep concern for this educational work. Walter Haldeman, Adam W. Miller, and Anna Koglin served under this arrangement. It soon became apparent, however, that knowledgeable workers needed to visit the Sunday schools and deal directly with the various problems they faced. Accordingly, in 1930 Pearl Johnson was employed as a field secretary. Others who gave itinerant service for Christian education during those early years were Esther Boyer, Adam W. Miller, Russell Olt, and Carl Kardatzke.

The work of the Board did not reach extensive proportions, however, until the early 1940s when it was able to employ full-time leadership. Irene Smith began as a part-time director and field worker in 1941 and later was named as the first full-time executive secretary. She resigned in 1944 to become professor of Christian education at what was then Pacific Bible College. R. Eugene Sterner served briefly as acting secretary, and in 1945 T. Franklin Miller was called to head the work of the Board of Christian Education. During his twenty-one years of service through this agency the role of Christian education in the total work of the Church of God was greatly extended. Miller's leadership was augmented by adding other trained personnel to provide specialized skills in such areas as field service, youth work, family life, children's work, worship, adult work, and leadership training. In 1966, when Miller was called to the presidency of Warner Press, Donald A. Courtney became executive secretary-treasurer for the Board. Under his direction further development and promotion of the church's ministry through education continued.

Training Leaders

Even before the organization of the Board of Christian Education several educationally-minded persons in the movement realized that the success of a Sunday school was largely dependent on the quality of its leadership. Consequently, one of the first projects for the new board was to tackle the problem of leadership training. This they did by sending out teachers to teach teachers. Sometimes individuals, sometimes teams, went out to area meetings and to local churches to conduct training classes, hold conferences, give demonstrations, and answer questions pertaining to leadership in Sunday schools and other phases of work in the church. Later this same technique was used in setting up laboratory schools and conducting workshops and clinics.

In the early 1930s the Board began participation in a program labeled as the Standard Leadership Training Curriculum which was outlined and accredited by what was then the International Council of Religious Education. Credits were offered at three levels of achievement. In 1932 over 500 such credits were awarded to persons who attended the required number of classes and did the specified reading. By 1949 the number of annual credits had reached 6,000 and in the 1950s the program peaked at 10,000 credits. Added to this program were home study courses and conferences at camp meetings and other assemblies. The Board established a lending library to enable any interested person to obtain needed reading and audio-visual material. A periodical for leaders entitled *Planning Creatively* was started in 1935 as a quarterly and later became a monthly. In 1959 the scope of the magazine was enlarged and its name was changed to *Christian Leadership*.

The development of programs for training lay leadership in local churches received a major boost in 1961-62 when the whole church participated in a special fund raising project captioned "Mission to Leaders." A total of $70,000 was raised, resulting in the extension of leadership training into several new areas and the addition of new staff members to implement the programs. Long before this, however, it was apparent that the task of training leaders for over 2,200 churches could never be accomplished from a national office, so encouragement and assistance in the development of state boards of Christian education had been under way for some time. In the late 1960s this decentralizing process gained new impetus with the formation of a program called Associates in Christian Education. By the mid-1970s there were almost 300 people across the country who had been solicited by their state boards to prepare themselves to become the volunteer trainers of leaders in local churches in their area.

Youth Work

The exact beginnings of organized youth work in the Church of God are not known. By the early 1900s separate meetings for youth were being held in some of the camp meetings. In 1924 the first International Young People's Convention was held on one day of the Anderson camp meeting and a precedent was established. In 1927 a committee was named to study the church's program for youth, and two years later the young people voted to hold their convention at a time other than the camp meeting. Accordingly, the seventh International Youth Convention was held in South Bend, Indiana in 1930. Thereafter a pattern of scheduling such a convocation every two years was followed. The 1970 convention in Louisville, Kentucky topped attendance records with a registration of almost 6,000.

Until 1943 all the leadership of the national youth work was volunteer service, but the program had developed to the point that a staff person was needed. A. Leland Forrest was named the first "field secretary." Funding of this office was difficult and other problems arose because youth work was unrelated to any other agency in the national structure. Consequently, in 1948 the youth voted to affiliate with the Board of Christian Education and Tom A. Smith became the first director under the new arrangement. Through this office a wide variety of program materials are made available to local youth leaders and, beyond the biennial conventions, many other national and international experiences such as work camps, seminars, and CARE labs are arranged and administered. In addition, an annual national youth convention during the Christmas holidays is planned and conducted by black young people in the Church of God.

Promotion with Purpose

The first intensive nation-wide effort to promote Christian education in the Church of God reformation movement came in 1934. A. T. Rowe, then general manager of the Gospel Trumpet Company, conceived the idea of starting a thousand new Sunday schools in a single year. With the help of Lestie Pletcher an advertising and direct mail promotional campaign was launched. The Gospel Trumpet Company offered to furnish free literature for the first quarter to every new Sunday school. Rowe wrote a pamphlet entitled, *One Thousand New Sunday Schools and How to Organize Them,* which was circulated widely. The Board of Christian Education gave support to the campaign. This venture did not completely reach the goal toward which it had aimed, but it was an outstanding success nevertheless. Six hundred new schools were organized during the year, over three hundred of them firmly enough to continue operation after the campaign was over. The *Yearbook* listing gives good evidence of the tremendous boost this effort gave to the educational work of the church. For 1933 1,072 Sunday schools reported. For 1934 the number had jumped to 1,575 and the total enrollment had increased by 6,000.

Another Christian education campaign in 1940 became the spearhead for a larger and more comprehensive program of promotion. The United Christian Advance was an adaptation of an interdenominational effort sponsored by the International Council of Religious Education, but carefully tailored to fit the Church of God movement and its needs. Under the direction of Irene Smith the Advance became the most vigorous promotional program of this nature in the history of the movement. As eventually developed the campaign focused attention on seven major goals: reach the unreached, train workers, launch new congregations, promote Christian reading, deepen spiritual life, Christianize the home, and enlist youth. Special committees outlined programs in these areas. Twenty-five books and pamphlets were published in the first two years of this five-year campaign, and concrete plans and check charts were distributed so that results could be evaluated. In addition to increasing attendance and improving the work of many local churches, this program brought the educational work of the church into sharp focus and made many leaders aware of the requirements for effective work.

The national Board of Christian Education observed its fiftieth anniversary in 1973 by calling a four-day consultation of sixty-three educators to analyze developments in their area of work and to help them plan ahead. The group formulated a list of thirty-seven goals for the future tasks of Christian education in the Church of God. They were agreed that the Sunday school is still a most significant vehicle for the church's outreach and that the quality of teaching which takes place there is crucial to success. Based on a conviction that the home is basic they reaffirmed a strong emphasis on family life education. The most specific outgrowth of the consultation was the launching of an attendance building program throughout the whole church. The General Assembly was asked to designate 1974 as the "Year of the Sunday School." Under the slogan of "Together We Can Reach More in '74" individual congregations were asked to enroll in this program which would provide them with resources and ideas for increasing attendance and upgrading their teaching. Almost 800 churches registered to participate. The response warranted a continuation of the program through 1975 with additional resources being provided for the improvement of the educational functions of each local church.

Even though educational work such as Sunday schools, vacation schools, and youth camps were slow in getting started in the Church of God reformation they have come to be one of the most significant aspects of the movement. The method of teaching was first accepted because of its great evangelistic potential. It is still proving to be the most effective means of outreach which the church is utilizing.

Points for Discussion

1. Why were Sunday schools opposed in the early days?
2. Why was the church so slow in developing any materials which could be used for teaching the various age groups?
3. Describe the most effective promotional campaigns for Christian education the church has carried on.
4. What has been the role of the Board of Christian Education in developing the ministry of teaching?
5. Does a strong emphasis on education mean that the church has lost its evangelistic zeal? Why?

Chapter VIII

TRAINING YOUTH FOR SERVICE

It has already been noted that the character of a religious reformation is determined in large part by the ideals which motivated it in the beginning and the character of the people who were captured by those ideals. A further observation needs to be made: the growth and continued success of that movement is dependent in large part on the quality and competence of the leadership it is able to attract and develop. Those who stand at the helm and guide the course of the movement after it has been launched and is on its way are just as important as the pioneers themselves. Of particular significance are the provisions which are made for training new leaders to supplement the work of those already established and to carry on after they are gone.

Even from the earliest days, the leaders felt concerned to enlist people competent in preaching, singing, and writing, and to a degree, at least, they recognized that those who went forth should be properly instructed in the content of the message as well as in the best ways of presenting it. Because this was a reform movement, however, protesting against the whole denominational system, quite naturally the leaders revolted against the accepted procedures of providing training for religious leaders. Moreover, the strong emphasis on direct leadership by the Holy Spirit tended to make a long period of theological and professional training seem unnecessary and a waste of time. Beyond that, such training was considered likely to make one proud and self-sufficient and less responsive to the leadings of the Spirit. Thus, though many of the early leaders were reasonably well educated, there soon developed a strong aversion to formal education for the Christian ministry.

Strong Language

The pioneers were not at all hesitant in expressing themselves in regard to ministers who received their training in the regular seminaries of that time. On October 1, 1883, Warner wrote in the *Trumpet:* "Of all the sects' loyal sons, that have been brought up in her damnable preacher factories, none are found fit for God's use." In another article in this same issue he defies "all the puffed-up sophistry of collegely wise, spiritually blind 'dumb dogs' " who teach that the day of miracles is past.

Further testimony is given by H. H. Mills, a minister who had gone through the prescribed period of formal training in one of the sect schools. He states: "That spirit of carnal pride and selfishness was fostered and stimulated by the college course in all its parts." For at least a period of years there seems to have been no defender of the minister who would look to the then existing institutions for his professional training.

Warner's attitude in these early years, stated positively, is perhaps best expressed in an article which appeared December 1, 1883. He wrote:

> The ability to talk the English language in its simplest form is all the education a soul needs to present Christ to dying sinners, when filled with the Comforter, and when destitute of Him', no amount of education can make a preacher of the Gospel.
>
> As to men prescribing a course of study as a condition for preaching the Gospel, that is the vilest form of popery.

Although Warner never altered his basic position, he did, in the later years of his life, come to see values in going further than simply being able to "talk the English language in its simplest form."

A Training School

In reviewing this vigorous opposition to "preacher factories" one is liable to get the idea that Warner and the other pioneers were opposed to any kind of training. That this was not the case is evidenced by the early acceptance of Sunday schools. Another indication that several of the early leaders were not opposed to education of the "right" type is the fact that a training school for workers was on the verge of being launched at the time of Warner's death. Although his condemnation of the "sect colleges" was just as vehement as ever, he was not at all averse to setting up a program of training within the framework of the reformation.

This idea of a training school was apparently an outgrowth of the educational program which had to be developed at Grand Junction in the early 1890s when provision was made for a number of the children of traveling evangelists to have a home there while their parents were away. The Grand Junction school district would not accept them in the public school since they were nonresidents, and so it was necessary to provide for their education. As some of the workers found value in attending these classes, particularly those in penmanship and music, it became apparent that there was demand for a more extensive program.

Warner's interest was kindled, and he took the lead in setting up the plans. In the fall of 1895 he wrote in the *Gospel Trumpet:*

> Frequently brethren have spoken and written to us concerning an opportunity to pursue a course in Bible study, preparatory to laboring in the vineyard of the Lord. A few days ago our heart was stirred very much with the duty of making an effort in this direction. Last Lord's Day we confessed our convictions, and a general impression has since then rested on the hearts of many brethren here that we ought to make a beginning of some kind. We have had a consultation before the Lord, and find all of one mind. And so we are safe in saying that something will be done in this good work.

Warner further indicated that arrangements could be made for about twelve students, but warned that none should come except "such as are thoroughly consecrated to God, dead to sin, utterly dead to 'youthful lusts,' and whose life in Christ is established and blameless." The course of study would be divided into three areas:

> First, Bible history and perhaps archaeology.
>
> Second, The critical study of the New Testament and lectures on prophecy.

Third, Experimental and spiritual truth. It is also hoped that music and elocution will be added.

The first meeting of these classes was scheduled for December 5, 1895, but Warner failed to appear. It was learned that he was ill so the group disbanded. Warner's death occurred a week later. On December 26 a notice appeared in the *Trumpet* stating, "Some have asked if we have a theological school here, We answer 'No,' neither do we expect to have." That was the end of the training school.

In the years that followed it seems to have been the tendency to apply all that had formerly been said about sectarian training schools to any which might be established by the movement itself. At various times during the next twenty years statements appeared which linked together educational training for the ministry, a salaried ministry, and the loss of divine insight and a prophetic voice. A 1905 article in the *Gospel Trumpet* (April 6) by D. O. Teasley, who was later to become the strong advocate of the Sunday school, expresses the attitude of the period. He writes:

All theological institutes and missionary training schools are run too much on the theoretical plan, which is detrimental to spirituality and tends to fill the head and empty the heart.

In this same article, however, Teasley defends what he calls the "experimental method" of training for the ministry. By this he meant that a young man who felt his call should spend some time in company with an older minister before going out in the work alone. He cites the biblical examples of Timothy and Titus who traveled with Paul during their youth. This method hardly needed defending, though, for it was for a number of years the most common way for a young man to get started in the ministry of the reformation.

The Road Back

Even while the opposition to formal training for leaders was at its highest, a particular technique for city evangelism was developing which was to lay the foundation for future colleges and seminaries. "Missionary homes" began to appear in the later 1890s as teams of workers went into various cities to conduct revival services, distribute literature, and help the needy. The first such home was probably the one in Chicago, started by Gorham Tufts in 1895. It operated as a rescue mission as well as an evangelistic center. In a few years other homes were established in New York, Kansas City, Oakland, Spokane, Portland, and many other cities.

These homes were all operated on a "faith" basis. The workers, many of whom were young people, received no salaries but were provided with food and other necessities. In almost every case an older minister was in charge, and others came for shorter periods. It was only natural that these eager young workers should seek counsel and guidance from those who were more experienced. This process is illustrated in a 1909 pamphlet describing the purposes of the New York City home. F. W. Heinly, who was then director, writes:

> This home offers an excellent place for the training and instruction of young workers whom God has called. No prescribed course of lessons is given, but . . . a number of established ministers and workers are always here, ready to give the young worker the benefit of their varied experiences in gospel work, expound the Scriptures, and present the best methods for the study of the Bible, how to win souls and conduct meetings in the most effectual way.

Informal counseling and study sessions soon developed into regular classes. Several of these homes later came to be designated as either Bible or missionary training schools. This was the case in New York, Kansas City, Spokane, Denver, and St. Paul Park. In many others also the educational work came to be a major part of the program. Classes also came to be a part of the schedule at the Gospel Trumpet Home after the publishing work was moved to Anderson, Indiana, in 1906.

During this time also there seems to have been a gradual softening of the harsh attitude toward all formal education, particularly if it were conducted under the proper auspices. In

June of 1912, for instance, an article appeared in the *Gospel Trumpet* entitled, "Advantages and Value of Education." H. W. Brooks was the author. After answering some of the current arguments against education he then presents some of the positive values, pointing out that much talent is lying dormant through lack of training and that souls are being lost because of the lack of knowledge and tact on the part of workers. He concludes by saying:

> Men and women upon whom God lays his hand for the ministry in their youth must be public speakers, singers, readers, and writers all the days of their life. Both God and man require this duty of them. They should qualify themselves to meet ably every obligation and to fill properly each duty required of them in their calling.

In 1914 a small-scale educational venture was launched in the Pacific Northwest. In connection with the Edmonds, Washington, camp meeting a ten-day "Gospel Institute" was held to give special training to workers in that area. Courses were offered in homiletics, pastoral methods, missions, Bible geography, history, music, English, speech and the Book of Revelation. E. G. Masters, the director, was assisted by G. W. Bailey, O. A. Burgess, and A. F. Gray. The institute was repeated in 1915, and in 1916 a similar program was carried on at the Colfax, Washington, camp meeting. Bailey and Burgess had already started holding classes at the Spokane Bible Institute. Between the years 1914 to 1919 a very comprehensive program of courses was offered. In 1920 the school was put under the control of the ministers of the area and moved to Boise, Idaho, where it operated for two years.

New Educational Ventures

While these training projects were in process of development in other parts of the country, there had also been some training activity among the workers of the Gospel Trumpet Company. Even though Warner's training school project at Grand Junction never materialized, those who lived in the Trumpet Home still met regularly for Bible study. This practice had continued during the years. In 1917, however, the general manager of the company, J. T. Wilson, felt that something more specific should be done to provide opportunities for training. Accordingly, he organized an "educational committee" which was to have charge of developing a program to train workers in the publishing office and others who wished to avail themselves of the opportunities offered.

This committee, composed of J. T. Wilson, H. A. Sherwood, R. R. Byrum, J. E. Campbell, and F. G. Smith, set to work immediately. In October of that year classes were being conducted on the first floor of the Trumpet Home. Most of the sixty-five students were people who lived in the Home and worked for the company. Perhaps no more than four or five devoted full time to their studies.

The development of Anderson Bible Training School was quite rapid. In 1919 John A. Morrison was called from a Colorado pastorate to become assistant principal. In 1923 he became principal. By 1925 the school was sufficiently strong to operate as an institution apart from the Gospel Trumpet Company. In that year Anderson Bible School and Seminary secured a charter from the state of Indiana and was set up as one of the agencies operating under the General Ministerial Assembly. A board of trustees of fifteen members was elected and Morrison's title was changed from principal to president. Russell Olt was named as dean.

Within another three years the school was asking for the privilege of offering a full four-year liberal arts college program. In 1928 the General Ministerial Assembly granted permission for this change to take place and the institution became Anderson College and Theological Seminary. This move was not made without opposition, however, for the next five years proved to be the most stormy of the institution's history. Many were not yet ready for the movement to sponsor a college-level program not specifically designed to train ministers and gospel workers. The climax of the opposition came in 1933 when the president's name came before the

Assembly for ratification. The opposition was strong and organized, but supporters of the college had also marshaled their forces to defend the step which had been taken. The president survived by a thirteen-vote margin, and the program of higher education was allowed to continue.

Following this controversy the college concentrated its energies on bringing its program up to the standard of other institutions. In 1937 the school was accredited by the Indiana Department of Education, and in 1946 full membership in the North Central Association of Colleges and Secondary Schools was granted. Subsequently, additional specialized accreditations were achieved in teacher education, music, social work, and nursing.

In 1958 Morrison retired from the presidency of the college after thirty-nine years of service to the institution. His successor was Robert H. Reardon, son of pioneer Church of God minister E. A. Reardon, The year 1958 also saw the death of Russell Olt who had been the college's dean for thirty-three years. Robert A. Nicholson was appointed to fill this position. Under the new team's leadership the college launched into a planned vigorous program of academic improvement and building. In 1961 the structure was altered by increasing the number of trustees to twenty, and in 1964 the official name of the school was shortened to Anderson College. By 1975 the campus consisted of about twenty main buildings on seventy-seven acres of land. Student enrollment had reached a total of 1,800 and the number of full-time faculty had increased to eighty.

Shortlived Ventures

The 1920s saw two other attempts to establish educational institutions. The first developed when the churches in eastern Kentucky became concerned about providing a Christian school for children and young people at the elementary and high school level. In 1927 they made their hope a reality and opened Winchester Academy in a newly constructed building on the church's campground in that city. W. T. Wallace was named president and Z. A. Horton served as dean. Enrollment was 45 the first year and increased to 136 the second year, but then things changed. The successful venture was cut short by problems arising from the economic crunch following the 1929 stock market crash. The school was forced to close in 1930.

In the Southwest another school was launched at about the same time. As early as 1927 there was interest in starting a church college in that area. By the following year approval for this project had been secured from the ministers of Texas, Oklahoma, and Louisiana, and a board of trustees had been selected. J. T. Wilson, then residing in Dallas, spearheaded this move and became the president of Warner Memorial University at Eastland, Texas. In 1929-1930 the first term of classes was conducted in temporary quarters, but by the following year two new buildings had been completed.

Unfortunately, the opening of this new institution also came just at the beginning of the great depression. The school had no regular means of support, and students were unable to find work in order to meet expenses. The situation became impossible, and so the university was forced to cease operations after three discouraging terms. Later attempts to revive the program were unsuccessful.

Rising Educational Concern

Since the mid-1930s concerned individuals and churches in various regions have taken the initiative in starting and developing six other educational institutions related to the Church of God. Two of these, Warner Pacific College and Gulf-Coast Bible College, have achieved national status through coming under the control of the General Assembly. By being admitted to the family of general agencies they receive financial support through the national World Service budget. The other four institutions are related to and supported largely by regional or state assemblies.

In the Pacific Northwest the early interest in educational programing mentioned earlier met with some reverses. The

Pacific Bible Institute was transferred from Boise to Seattle in 1922. After only one year in the new location the ministers voted to discontinue the school temporarily because of low enrollment and high cost. A dozen years later this "temporary" suspension came to an end and active measures were initiated to revive the training program in Seattle. Two years later, in 1937, the school gained regional support and was incorporated by the Northwest Ministerial Assembly as Pacific Bible College. It was relocated in Spokane in the facilities of the old missionary home. A. F. Gray was again named as president. Because of increasing enrollment and the desire for a more central location the college was moved to Portland, Oregon in 1940 and Otto F. Linn was called to be dean. In 1959 the name of the school was changed to Warner Pacific College and in 1961 the institution received accreditation as a liberal arts college by its regional accrediting association. Following Gray's retirement as president in 1957, Milo L. Chapman was named to this position. He was succeeded by Louis F. Gough in 1962 and in 1966 E. Joe Gilliam was called to be president of the institution. By the mid 1970s student enrollment had reached approximately 450.

In Western Canada two schools were started in the early 1930s: an English school in Edmonton and a German school in Medicine Hat, Alberta. In 1934 these two joined and located at Ferintosh, Alberta. The following year the school was relocated in Camrose and began functioning as Alberta Bible Institute. Harry C. Gardner was the first president and served the school in this capacity for almost a quarter of a century. Others who have headed the Canadian school are Gordon A. Schieck, Thomas A. Hall, Milton J. Chugg, and A. F. Irving. In 1973 David W. Davis was called to the position. Although enrollment in the school has never been large, numbering usually fewer than thirty students, its contribution in training leadership has been most significant.

Texas was to be the location of the next venture in higher education. In the fall of 1953 South Texas Bible Institute began operation in Houston with Max R. Gaulke as president. By 1955 the curriculum had been expanded and the school became Gulf-Coast Bible College. It functioned under the sponsorship of the Texas Ministerial Assembly until 1968 when the school became a general agency of the national church. It was also in 1968 that the college became a full member of the Accrediting Association of Bible Colleges. Student enrollment had reached approximately 300 by the mid 1970s. Upon Gaulke's retirement in 1975 John W. Conley became president.

In 1954 the churches in southern California made provision for the launching of a new college at Arlington with C. Herbert Joiner, Jr., as president and Albert J. Kempin as dean. In 1960 the school was moved to Long Beach, California but retained the name Arlington College. In 1961 George H. Ramsey became president of the institution. He was succeeded by Dewayne B. Bell in 1963. Five years later the college affiliated with Azusa Pacific College, a school which had been brought into being three years earlier by the merger of two older evangelical colleges. Thus the Association of the Church of God of southern California became one of the sponsoring units of this interdenominational school with proportionate representation on the board of trustees and faculty. Arlington College president Bell became assistant to the president of Azusa Pacific College. By the mid 1970s around fifty of the college's 900 students were from the Church of God.

Bay Ridge Christian College began operation at Kendleton, Texas in 1961 after a thwarted attempt to launch the school a year earlier in Mississippi. This educational project, designed specifically for the training of black leaders in the rural South, was developed largely by J. Horace Germany who became president of the institution. Combining academic and religious training with the teaching of agricultural skills, the school utilizes a 234 acre farm and a large dairy herd. Its operation is controlled by a board of trustees elected by the Southern Association of the Church of God, a voluntary assembly of ministers and lay people, mostly black, who meet annually on the campus of the school. After fifteen years of operation student enrollment had reached a total of sixty.

Warner Southern College had its beginning in 1968 on a newly constructed campus at Lake Wales, Florida. Concern for having a Church of God school in the Southeast had been expressed twenty years earlier at the time of the organizing of the regional Southern Convention. Attempts by this Convention to develop extension centers of Anderson College did not prove successful so in 1964 a group of congregations in the South formed the Southeastern Association of the Church of God for the purpose of establishing and sponsoring a college. Trustees selected by this association named Leroy M. Fulton as president and Leslie W. Ratzlaff as dean. The college's enrollment by 1975 had reached a total of approximately 200 students.

Coordination and Planning

By the late 1940s, when existing educational institutions were expanding to take advantage of the post World War II boom in student enrollments and there was increasing interest in various parts of the country in starting new church colleges, several leaders in the Church of God became aware of the need for some national planning and strategizing in the field of higher education. Accordingly, a study committee in this area was proposed and was authorized by the General Assembly. After several years of study this committee in 1957 recommended the establishment of a permanent Commission on Christian Higher Education. The following year the Assembly approved the proposal and the Commission was constituted.

This Commission, composed of representatives from existing colleges related to the Church of God and six members elected by the Assembly, was authorized to perform a coordinative function among the educational institutions involved and to guide the development of a total higher education program in the church. It would be available for special assignments from the Assembly in this area, a provision which the Assembly utilized in 1972 when it assigned the Commission the task of making a thorough and extensive study of theological education and ministerial training in the Church of God. In general, the Commission would be a liason between the colleges and the church.

A Professionally Trained Ministry

The impact of a better educated constituency in the movement eventually created some demand for a more professionally trained ministry. By the 1930s several of the church's youth were pursuing graduate studies, and during the next decade a significant number of future leaders were enrolled in seminaries and graduate schools across the country. It was becoming apparent that there was a need to provide professional graduate training for ministry within the Church of God. In 1950 the trustees of Anderson College authorized the establishment of a seminary in conjunction with the college, sharing the same president but having its own dean. The first dean of Anderson School of Theology was Earl L. Martin. In 1953 he was succeeded by Adam W. Miller who served until his retirement in 1962. Gene W. Newberry followed in this office for the next twelve years until 1974 when Barry L. Callen was named as his successor.

From its beginning the School of Theology offered a standard three-year graduate program for the professional training of ministers and granted what came to be the Master of Divinity degree. Later (1967), the two-year Master of Religious Education was added, and still later (1973) a number of other specialized graduate degrees in religion were added to the offerings. The seminary received accreditation by the Association of Theological Schools in 1966. A new School of Theology building on the Anderson College campus was built in 1961 with a new chapel and other additions completed in 1975. By the mid 1970s student enrollment had reached 140.

This review of the development of higher education in the Church of God reveals a very dramatic change of viewpoint and a substantial realignment of concerns. From a stance of opposition to formal advanced training in the mid 1910s the church moved in six decades to the point of giving support to seven colleges and a seminary with a combined budget of almost thirteen million dollars.

Points for Discussion

1. On what basis was formal education for ministers opposed in the early years of the Church of God reformation?
2. In the period when there were no educational institutions, how were leaders trained?
3. To what extent does the present interest in education constitute a reversal of previous viewpoints?
4. Give an account of the major educational ventures in the Church of God.
5. Is education necessarily antagonistic to spirituality? Why?

CHAPTER IX

A CONCERN FOR NEIGHBORS

The fact that reform movements in Christianity have tended to concentrate on the particular points where changes were desired and have neglected to emphasize other aspects of the Christian faith is well known. In a very real sense this kind of concentrated emphasis characterized the earliest period of the Church of God reformation. The tremendous concern the pioneers had for calling people out of sectarian division, for proclaiming the unity of the church, and for preaching the necessity of personal holiness left little time for giving major attention to such matters as improving social conditions, ministering to the underprivileged, or even extending their evangelistic effort among neglected peoples on the North American continent.

A close study of the early period of the movement's history, however, reveals that these areas were not entirely neglected. There is evidence of a surprisingly large number of concerns beyond the purely reformatory and evangelistic. The very earliest issues of the *Gospel Trumpet,* for instance, state the subscription price and then add, "Free to the Poor." It was not uncommon in those early years for the *Trumpet* to print appeals for help from needy people or groups. A note appearing in the July 15, 1890, issue illustrates this concern:

> Sister Jennie Davidson of Olivet, wishes to thank the several kind brethren who responded to her appeal in the *Trumpet* some time ago, for aid to release her home of the mortgage upon it. She received in all up to time of writing $745.

Even earlier than this, in November of 1881, the attention of *Trumpet* readers was called to a group of about two hundred homesteaders who had settled on government land too late in the season to plant crops. Some were actually starving. Not only was it suggested that the "saints" send donations to these people but also that those who had property might secure a mortgage on it in order to obtain money to loan to the unfortunate settlers. Although the response to this appeal is not known, it does indicate a real interest even at this early period in helping persons in dire need.

Wider Concerns

Concern also for a social ministry beyond the serving of needy individuals was evidenced quite early. In the year 1893 one of the movement's leading evangelists, Sebastian Michels, became strongly motivated to provide Christian care for homeless children. He secured an adequate facility in South Haven, Michigan, and established an orphanage. While this project was in its early stages it was strongly promoted through the *Gospel Trumpet,* and regular reports of progress were printed. Later, however, some of the other ministers apparently felt that caring for needy children was not really evangelistic work, so they brought severe criticism on Michels for neglect of his calling. In spite of this censure he continued to operate the home for a number of years. It ceased functioning after the publishing work was moved from the area.

It is well to note, however, that over seven decades later the movement once again became involved nationally in an institutional-type child care project. In the early 1960s a Kentucky Church of God couple, Robert and Ruby Kitchen, became deeply concerned about children in distress. They began a local child-care program which was to become Hope Hill Children's Home. Their first new building was completed in 1962 and by the end of 1965 they were legally incorporated and licensed by the state. Under the direction of S. Richard Dillon, services were expanded beyond child care to also include child placing and family guidance. They solicited funds nationally, mostly from Church of God congregations, and developed a very adequate facility on 185 acres of land. In 1974 the Hope Hill corporation board relinquished its control and management of the home and turned it over, debt free, to the national Board of Church Extension and Home Missions. In accepting this responsibility for the church the Board, in a sense, validated the concern which Sebastian Michels had felt so keenly many years before.

The missionary home program, mentioned earlier as primarily an evangelistic technique, also had a help-the-needy aspect. The earliest of these homes, established in Chicago in 1895 by Gorham Tufts, was started as a rescue mission. For a number of years a full city mission program of providing food, temporary shelter, and needed clothing was maintained for the city's unfortunates. Also a free employment agency gave assistance in rehabilitation. Some of the other missionary homes likewise had modified relief programs in conjunction with their evangelistic work.

One of the first concerns of this nature which could be considered national in scope was care for the aged. In the same year that the Gospel Trumpet Company plant was build in Anderson, Indiana (1907), an old people's home was also built. This home was designed primarily to provide care for aged ministers and gospel workers, but others were admitted as space and funds were available. For the first few years this project was operated as a department of the Gospel Trumpet Company, but the management was later turned over to a group of individuals known as the Anderson Old People's Home Association. This arrangement did not prove satisfactory, so in 1918 the operation of the home was again taken over by the Company. In 1920 an additional home in St. Paul Park, Minnesota, formerly operated by some of the Scandinavian brethren, was also taken over. These two homes for the aged continued to function for a number of years as benevolent agencies of the church. Financial difficulties and changing conditions eventually forced both to close.

Another evidence of interest in needy neighbors was the publishing work for the blind. This was begun as a private venture around 1906 by Grace DeFore, who was herself sightless, in California. In 1910 she moved to Anderson and her work became a department of the Gospel Trumpet Company. In 1913 a *Gospel Trumpet* for the blind began publication and in 1917 the *Sunday School Monthly* was started. The latter publication was advertised for a time as the only Sunday school quarterly in raised type being published in the United States.

Missions at Home

In the earliest phases of outreach in this reformation no distinction was made between home and foreign missions. In fact, the first missionary board was designated as the Board of Home and Foreign Missions. By 1917 the interest in overseas work had become so great and its management so complex that the Board asked the General Ministerial Assembly for permission to drop home missions from its responsibility. In the reorganization of that year the request was granted. This change did not really alter the work of the Board very much, for, with the exception of the Spanish work, very little had been done up to this time which could be classed as home missions.

In June of 1920 a new agency called the Board of Church Extension and Home Missions came into being. Its chief promoter and first president was J. T. Wilson. As implied in its name, this board was given specific responsibility in two areas. Church extension has to do with the planting of new congregations in neglected areas and the strengthening of churches not yet able to carry on without outside assistance. Home missions has to do with work among immigrants, Indian Americans, Mexicans, migrant workers, and people living in underprivileged areas. The field, in general, covers the continent of North America with the exception of Mexico.

For the first several years of its existence this new board was occupied primarily in church extension work. There were many sections of the country and certain strategic population centers into which the ''natural'' processes of evangelistic outreach had not carried the message of this reformation. To the task of extending the work into these areas the Board first directed itself and new churches were planted in Boston, Omaha, Atlanta, and

Dallas, all within a few years. These congregations were expected to serve as centers for further evangelistic effort. A revolving loan fund was established also to help new congregations get started and to give assistance to growing churches needing to expand or make improvements. Over two thousand such loans totaling more than $22.5 million were made in the period from 1920 to 1974. Church extension work has been furthered through the years also by giving guidance in cooperative evangelism, providing architectural consultation service, assisting state and district boards of evangelism, and in conducting regional personal evangelism clinics.

Mission to Mexican Americans

The oldest venture into the area later described as home missions was among the Spanish-speaking people of the Southwest. In 1891 a former Methodist minister by the name of B. F. Elliott felt impressed, while preaching in Santa Barbara, California, to take the message of the reformation to the Mexicans. He knew nothing of the Spanish language at the time but quickly learned it and within a short time was able to preach in Spanish. He went across the border into lower California and eventually was able to establish a publishing work at La Paz. In 1908 the D. W. Pattersons joined Elliott and his wife, and the outlook for a good work in that area seemed very promising. Within a short time, however, rumors of revolution made it seem expedient to leave Mexico so they moved to El Paso, Texas. Here they were joined by L. Y. Janes and his wife who also were deeply concerned about developing a Spanish-language ministry. With three couples on the scene this appeared to be a very auspicious arrangement for rapid development, but the opportunity dissolved rather suddenly when the Elliotts began an independent operation and the other two families moved on to other places.

In 1908 M. F. Tafolla, who was already a Christian minister, came in contact with the Church of God through a *Gospel Trumpet* given him by a German brother from Buda, Texas. In the following years Tafolla preached to Mexican people in Texas, California, and Mexico, but he did not organize any congregations. In 1920 he concentrated on San Antonio and a work was started.

It was also in 1920 that the Spanish Evangelical Association was formed with offices in Los Angeles, California. Although this association had no direct connection with any of the general agencies of the church, it had the backing of the national leaders. The purpose of this group was to encourage capable people to prepare for gospel work in the Spanish language. They formed a subsidiary known as the Spanish Literature Company for the printing and distribution of Spanish literature. B. O. Bertelson was in charge of the Los Angeles office.

Within the next few years all of this work among the Mexicans in the United States was brought within the responsibility of the Home Missions Board, and more workers were made available for this ministry in Spanish. In 1930, for instance, following a revival by Tafolla in Los Angeles, the Bertelsons started a Sunday school for Mexicans. They had no regular minister for the church, however, until the following year when the Board sent the A. T. Maciels to assist in this work. A church building was erected in 1937, and the congregation, under Maurice Caldwell, became self-supporting in 1951. Samuel Colunga became pastor in 1954 and in 1959 Fidel Zamarano, who was later to become also the speaker for the Christian Brotherhood Hour—Spanish, assumed leadership of this group.

In the American Southwest other Spanish-speaking congregations were later established in Corpus Christi, Somerset, and Houston, Texas and in Albuquerque, New Mexico. Other mission workers in this area have included the Elsworth Palmers, Lloyd Butler, the Paul Chappels, the Albert Bentleys, the Warren Kinions, the Edward Oldhams, the William Westlakes, the Keith Planks, the George Geiwitzs, and the Louis Geiwitzs. Several additional capable Mexican-American leaders have arisen to fill places of major responsibility in the churches in this area. Among those who have held or continue to hold positions of leadership are Gregorio Casteneda, Raphael Compos, Luz Gonzales, Ernesto Lopez, Lorenzo Mondragon, Adolfo Pesquera, Lorenzo Ramos, Joe Salinas, Annie Tafolla, and Marciano Yates. L. Y. Janes extended the ministry to Spanish-speaking people by establishing Christian Unity Press in Corpus Christi. In 1948 a monthly periodical, *La Trompeta,* began publication from this press with Annie Tafolla as its first editor. By 1973 the scope of coverage and the circulation of this magazine had extended to include all of Spanish-speaking Latin America and its place of publication was moved to Puerto Rico with Earl Carver as editor.

The influx of Latin American immigrants to the American east coast led to the establishment of Spanish-speaking congregations in that area. One of these is in Miami, Florida. Elsworth Palmer, who had been a missionary in Cuba, was forced to leave when diplomatic relations between that country and the United States were broken by the Castro revolution. In 1960 he followed the Cuban refugees to Florida and established a ministry among them. Another congregation developed in Washington, D.C. In 1963 a group of Latin American evangelicals began holding services. Within a short time their ministry expanded to include people from fifteen nations. During the civil rights disturbances of 1968 the building where they were meeting was burned and they accepted the offer of the National Memorial Church of God to use their facilities as long as needed. The ultimate result was that this group under the leadership of their pastor, Roberto Peon Oliva, became a Spanish-speaking congregation of the Church of God, continuing to share facilities with the National Memorial congregation.

Since 1954 the leaders of these congregations have been able to plan together and communicate with each other through the Spanish American Council of the Church of God. Initiated and sponsored by the Board of Church Extension and Home

Missions this Council has strongly encouraged the involvement of Hispanic-American leadership in all phases of this ministry among Spanish-speaking peoples in the United States. Until 1970 the Home Missions Board also had had the responsibility for developing the work of the church in Mexico, but at that time it became apparent that it would be well to coordinate all Latin American work outside the United States under the Missionary Board.

Native American Work

On February 12, 1875, D. S. Warner visited an Omaha encampment in Nebraska. That night he wrote in his diary: "May the kind providence of God yet elevate this poor distressed people to a higher plane of intellectual, moral, and religious development." It was not, however, until March of 1939 that active steps were taken by the Church of God to do evangelistic work among these native Americans.

The first Indian American mission was on the Tulalip Reservation in the state of Washington. It was started because Rollo Maulsby, who was leasing land from the Tulalips, became burdened about taking the gospel to them. He began asking for help. In 1939 the Home Missions Board sent the J. Frank Shaws to begin this ministry. After a discouraging period in which they met with practically no response the Shaws were finally able to establish a Sunday school. In 1943 they left to do similar work in Toppenish, Washington, and the Leland Harrimans took over the Tulalip work. When they left in 1947 native American B. Adam Williams and his wife became pastors of this reservation church.

At the same time the first mission was established in Washington another was begun at Wounded Knee, South Dakota, among the Sioux Indians on the Pine Ridge Reservation. This work was begun by students from the Gordon (Nebraska) Bible School. Later the Herbert Petersons became the first resident missionaries. Subsequently the Dennis Tylers and the Orville Lansberrys served this mission church at

Wounded Knee. Following the demonstrations there by the American Indian Movement in 1973 it appeared advisable to secure native American leadership. In 1974 the Mark Black Calfs became pastors of this congregation.

In the 1940s and 1950s the Indian work was extended to stations in Lapwai, Idaho; Crow Agency, Montana; Alliance, Gordon, and Scottsbluff, Nebraska; Cherokee Hills, Oklahoma; and Celilo Falls, Oregon. In 1969 the first formal outreach of the Church of God among the Navajos was started in Arizona. Bahe and Mabel Woodman, native Navajo leaders, began the work which became the Klagetoh Shelter Mission consisting of a central church and three preaching outposts served by young Navajo leaders.

In addition to those already mentioned the following people have had an active part in this ministry to Indian Americans: The James Koles, the Boyd Koles, the Harold Wrights, the Norman Hauses, the Harry F. Martins, the John E. Millers, the Wiley Halls, Lois McKinney, Vern Pickard, the Earl Baileys, the Elmer Hosslers, the John GrosVenors, and the Keith Planks. Leroy Falling, an Indian educator, has given strong lay leadership to the work of the church among his people.

On the Geographic Frontiers

The Church of God reformation was extended to Alaska through the persistence of the wife of a gold prospector. In the late 1920s Mrs. A. O. Wells, who had heard this message in the States, began writing to friends and to the leaders in Anderson of the tremendous possibilities in this rapidly developing territory. The fact that she got no help and little encouragement for the first several years did not deter her in the least. She kept witnessing in every way she could and kept writing letters. In 1934 E. F. Adcock, then secretary of the Home Missions Board, went to Alaska to investigate. He found the opportunities even greater than Mrs. Wells had pictured them. The following year the D. W. Pattersons were sent to Alaska as home missionaries.

The first congregation was established at Palmer in the Matanuska Valley, which was at that time just being opened to settlement. The Pattersons also began a work in Anchorage. Buildings were erected in both places and solidly founded congregations eventually developed. Within a few years groups were assembled and church buildings constructed in Sutton, Juneau, Fairbanks, and Kodiak. A second church was established in Anchorage and the outreach has been extended to Wrangell and Kenai. To further their evangelistic concern, as well as to afford an opportunity for these widely scattered churches to join in a period of fellowship, the leaders launched an annual camp meeting. To accommodate this and other programs they secured and developed a facility known as Camp Challenge.

Of particular interest in the Alaska work is the development of two children's homes under the sponsorship of the church or church people. Sanford and Clara Davis began operating a home in the Matanuska Valley, but later moved to Fairbanks, taking the project with them. After the Davises left the valley, the churches in the Palmer-Anchorage area arranged to open a children's home in January of 1953, with the Chester Cantleys as superintendents. Changing conditions in the years following statehood made it no longer feasible to operate these orphanages, but the Alaska mission churches served this need while it existed.

In addition to those who came to minister in this frontier area as home missionaries under sponsorship of the Board there were a great number of other people whose leadership contributed to the development of the work in Alaska. Some of those who have had a significant part in planting and nourishing the congregations in this area are: George Geiwitz, James Austin, John Marshall, Herman Beyer, Judson Masters, Russell Wilson, Albert Compton, Jarrell Frazee, Wesley Lancaster, Ervin Cultice, Paul Kendall, William Miller, Ken Richards, Dwight Nelson, George Majors, Richard Swank, Jack Hope, Donald Unsell, Richard Lawrenz, Marvin Matthews, and many others.

In Hawaii the Church of God had made some contacts earlier but had no organized work until 1955. A chance meeting of three couples who discovered they were all associated with the movement led to the beginning of meetings and eventually a call to the mainland for leadership. The Carl Rileys from Washington responded in the summer of 1956 and the Aina Haina church was organized. The group was small at first, consisting largely of military service personnel and students, and the problems of acquiring facilities and maintaining pastoral leadership were great. Eight different pastors served the congregation in its first sixteen years. A second congregation was attempted in the late 1960s at Waipahu but it was not able to achieve sufficient financial strength to survive.

In 1968 the Aina Haina congregation requested financial assistance from the Missionary Board and an arrangement for providing leadership was agreed upon. In 1970 these cooperative arrangements were transferred to the Board of Church Extension and Home Missions. Other persons who have served as pastoral leaders in Hawaii are the John D. Croses, the Nick Van Der Veurs, the Edgar Buschs, the Proctor Barbers, the Jerome Humphries, the Brice Caseys, the Ernesto Babas, the T. M. Ramsays and the John H. Williams. Among the many strong lay leaders have been the Bill Wrights, the Curtis Loewens, and the Kenneth Smiths.

Other Ministries

To mention all the neighborly concerns which have been evidenced in the Church of God reformation would be next to impossible, but a few more projects in which there has been national participation will indicate the scope of interest. In 1939 Mr. and Mrs Lee Francis moved into the eastern Kentucky mountain community known as Yellow Rock. They learned there had never been a church in this neighborhood, so they secured a dilapidated school building and started a Sunday school. The following year Naomi Randall came into the region and became aware that many more communities were in the same condition as Yellow Rock had been. In the next few years congregations were established at Blaines Branch, Millers Creek, and May's School. Pine Crest Youth Center was opened in 1948, making it possible to carry on a full camping program and to have a place for rural pastors' conferences, missionary retreats, and leadership institutes of various kinds. The Simon Robinsons, the Robert Sperows, the Willard Armeys, the Jerry Yoders and the Gene Mortons have served in this work.

In the 1960s it became apparent that the church as a whole needed to give more attention to its ministry in urban areas. The Board of Church Extension began special programming in this area and added two staff persons to implement extensive plans. In 1970 the whole church launched a special $150,000 fund raising effort called "Mission USA" which was designed to enable both persons and congregations in needy areas to extend and upgrade their ministerial service through education, planning, and cooperative action. The successful conclusion of this project the following year made it possible to provide many scholarships to train potential leaders from minority groups, to implement a variety of service programs, and to enable congregations in cities such as Detroit, Chicago, Denver, Toledo, Portland, and San Francisco to reach out into new ministries like Neighborhood House, Pinewood House, East Side Detroit Mission, Indian Center, and various other cooperative ventures in alleviation of human distress.

Coordination of Efforts

Along with urban concerns, the 1960s brought also an increasing awareness that a church faithful to the gospel must concern itself with such social problems as civil rights, racism, poverty, alcoholism, drug abuse, abortion, war, and multiplied other issues. Many congregations and almost all of the national church agencies responded in some way to the urgent demands of the time. Hundreds of students from the church's colleges spent summers in volunteer service all over the world, educational and humanitarian programs were implemented locally and nationally, and interracial consultations helped the church face up to certain imbalances within its own structures. To provide a vehicle for coordinating these various service and witness activities and to assure that human need responsibilities would be kept continually before the church a permanent Commission on Social Concerns was created by the General Assembly in June of 1964.

This Commission, composed of fifteen elected members and a representative from each of the general agencies, was deliberately designed to be multiracial and broadly typical of the whole church. In addition to its task of coordination and lifting up of proper Christian concerns for personal, social, and civic righteousness, the Commission was charged with the responsibility to "carefully study the great issues confronting Christians in today's world and to propose appropriate ways for Christians to discharge their responsibility individually and corporately." Subsequent annual reports from the Commission indicate a serious attempt to fulfill its obligation.

In addition to what is done in this area "officially" by designated church agencies there is also a vast amount of service to needy people by individuals whose concern has been deep and whose giving has been great because they have believed that Jesus meant it when he said, "Love thy neighbor as thyself."

Points for Discussion

1. How did some of the early leaders show their concern for people's physical needs?
2. How did it happen that many of these concerns were handled through the Gospel Trumpet Company?
3. How do you account for the decline in interest in the Church of God for institutions such as orphanages and old people's homes?
4. Describe the aims of the Board of Church Extension and Home Missions and name some of its major activities.
5. Should the Church of God be participating in other projects, such as hospitals and clinics? Should these serve only Church of God people?

CHAPTER X

AN INTERCULTURAL FELLOWSHIP

The Church of God reformation was born and had its initial development at a time when the character of America's population was changing rapidly. The first and most obvious feature of this change was the transformed status of almost eight million Americans of African descent who had been slaves and who, only a short time before the beginning of this movement, had become "freedmen." There was really no way for any group with a nationwide identity to avoid some involvement in the issues of race relations and civil rights. This was particularly true of religious groups, for the ex-slaves were a religious people. By the time of the Civil War many thousands of them were active Christians, worshiping either with their masters or in congregations affiliated with their masters' denominations.

After emancipation it would have seemed logical that the freed Blacks would have continued in these same churches. But such was not the case. The context was completely changed. The old paternalistic relationship of whites and Blacks was no longer acceptable to either. Almost immediately the Blacks began forming their own denominations, usually retaining the family name of the parent group but with added adjectives to affirm clearly their distinctiveness. New denominations appeared with names such as Colored Primitive Baptist, African Methodist Episcopal, National Baptist Convention, or Colored Methodist Episcopal. These were segregated black churches; most of them were formed between 1865 and 1895.

Among the Black People

A new religious movement being formed in this period when racial separateness was in the air would hardly be expected to take a strong interracial stance. In effect, however, this is what the Church of God did even though it was not widely proclaimed or even verbalized. A careful search of the writings of D. S. Warner, for instance, reveals practically no stated concern for the plight of the black people nor any special plea to evangelize among them. Even so, as the message went forth it very early found a response among people of African heritage.

Almost from the beginning, dating back at least to 1886, Black Americans have been a significant part of the movement's history. The first known black leader was a woman, Jane Williams, pastor of a congregation in Charleston, South Carolina. Her identification with the movement was really the beginning of the Church of God in that state. Charleston became a center from which the work spread to all the other southeastern states. Black and white leaders worked hand in hand as other congregations were established in the South and in the North as well.

The number of black ministers increased quite rapidly. In a study of black churches in the Church of God (*An Introduction to the Negro Churches in the Church of God Reformation Movement,* Shining Light Survey Press, 1957), James Earl Massey identified over thirty black leaders in the movement by 1900; a decade later this number had increased to 150. Among these earliest black ministers were prominent leaders such as R. J. Smith, Charles H. Hill, C. T. Benjamin, Beatrice Sapp, Daniel F. Oden, and J. D. Smoot.

One of the great attractions to the Church of God movement for black people was its teaching on Christian unity. For them this implied a fellowship transcending all barriers, racial as well as sectarian. Both Blacks and whites sought to make this ideal a reality. There are many accounts of interracial meetings being held in defiance of prevailing customs and even laws. But the cultural pressures were great and the ideal of full racial unity began to crumble. In 1909 two interracial congregations in the North, Pittsburg and New York City, were each divided along the color line. The following year the same thing happened in St. Louis, and by 1915 similar separations had taken place in Chicago and Detroit.

During this same period, probably around 1912, black leaders reported a racial confrontation at the international camp meeting in Anderson. White leaders are said to have told the Blacks that too many of them were coming to the meeting, thus hindering many whites from coming and being saved. It would be better, they thought, if Blacks were to find a suitable place and hold their own camp meeting.

The stage was set for splitting the movement along racial lines, and that is what happened—almost. Without any deliberate planning or design a modified unity was maintained while a separate structure was allowed to develop. The unofficial arrangement which emerged preserved the concept of an open fellowship with unrestricted participation by all ministers, white or black, in the general work of the movement. At the same time the Blacks were free, and apparently were encouraged, to develop whatever of their own structures they desired. The inevitable result was a complex situation—a church body which was largely segregated at the local level and unified at the national level, with a satellite national structure generated by the segregated black churches and independent of the general national structure. In addition, separate black and white ministerial assemblies developed in most of the states in the South and some in the North.

Quite independent of any of these developing barriers between the races a black minister was able to procure a plot of land near West Middlesex, Pennsylvania which was to play a large role in the development of the Church of God among black people. Elisha A. Wimbush, a former Baptist who had taken his stand with the Church of God and was pastor of a congregation in Sharon, Pennsylvania, had long dreamed of a place in a beautiful setting where people could gather for worship and praise. He found the right spot. In rather primitive conditions the first camp meeting was held in 1917. Although this camp was envisioned purely as a place for spiritual refreshment with no original racial concern whatsoever, the annual meetings held there were to become the vehicle for the development of a variety of churchly structures parallel in many ways to the general agencies in Anderson, Indiana. These were headed by a central organization designated eventually as the "National Association of the Church of God." West Middlesex became the black "headquarters." The physical facilities of the camp were improved through the years, with great credit for this to longtime manager Joseph Crosswhite, Sr., who retired in 1960 after 33 years of service. In 1974 a new tabernacle was completed at a cost of $237,000, making this a modern and very beautiful center for religious activity.

Throughout this whole development of segregation Blacks continued to participate in the general work of the church. Black ministers never lost the right of membership in the General Assembly and many attended. Most of the national agencies sought to have at least one black member on their board. One or more black speakers, such as J. D. Smoot, S. P. Dunn, and Raymond S. Jackson, always appeared on the program of the international convention. All the schools and colleges of the church have been open to Blacks and many have taken advantage of the opportunity. In the heat of the vigorous civil rights movement of the 1960s, however, these procedures were judged to be quite inadequate—"tokenism," "window dressing" with "representative" Blacks for display. A "Black Caucus" was held and a delegation visited Anderson to call attention to various practices in national offices judged to be racist and discriminatory.

The white leaders listened, and through the later 1960s and 1970s many changes were effected. Blacks were secured for administrative positions in the national agencies, for faculty and staff positions in the colleges, and increasingly as writers for church publications. Chicago pastor Marcus H. Morgan was elected in 1971 as chairman of the Executive Council. The following year Cauthion T. Boyd, Jr., a retired army chaplain colonel, was chosen president of the Missionary Board. In 1975 Edward L. Foggs moved from a staff position with the Board of Church Extension to become Associate Executive Secretary of the Executive Council and Thomas J. Sawyer came from the faculty of Anderson College to be the Associate Secretary of the Missionary Board.

On the National Association side of the ledger there were also significant changes. In several states the separate black assemblies were merged with the white assemblies. The missionary activity of the two separate boards was merged, and other parallel functions began being coordinated. The *Shining Light Survey,* a periodical edited by Evans Marshall and published by the black brethren since 1933, reports and promotes the work of the general causes as well as those related directly to Blacks.

By the mid-1970s there were approximately 20,000 Blacks associated with the Church of God. They worship in 430 predominantly black congregations. This means that around twelve percent of the constituency of the movement and eighteen percent of the congregations are black. Growth studies indicate that increases in these churches account for a great percentage of the recent growth of the movement as a whole.

European Immigrants

During the developing years of the Church of God movement the population constituency of the American nation also was being altered drastically by forces without as well as within. The primary reason for this change was the great influx of immigrants from other countries. In the decade between 1880 and 1890 more than five million people entered America's ports, and in the next ten-year period another three and one-half million arrived. The high point of immigration was reached in 1905 when more than one million foreigners came in a single year. In every nation in Europe as well as in other parts of the world the United States of America was hailed as "the land of opportunity," and great numbers of people responded. The many nationalities, the various cultures, and the differing languages all became a part of a new life in a new world. The fusion of all these elements in a single society made the term *melting pot* a very appropriate description of America in the early twentieth century.

Because these immigrants came in such great numbers and in such a short span of years they tended to settle in groups and to retain much of their former culture. Consequently, in the America of this period there were many areas, both urban and rural, where the language and customs of a particular foreign country were preserved without much change. This quite naturally included religious loyalties. Since most of the immigrants came from countries with state churches, usually everyone in a particular area would be affiliated with the same church. The Scandinavians, for instance, would be mostly Lutheran, the Germans would be either Lutheran or Reformed or perhaps Mennonite; and the Slavs, Poles, Italians, and Irish would be largely Roman Catholic. The Greeks were, of course, chiefly Orthodox.

As the Church of God movement expanded into various sections of the country it was only natural that it should encounter some of these nationality groups. The leaders felt no hesitancy whatever in seeking converts among these people, for the message of the reformation seemed just as applicable here as elsewhere. By 1920 a significant work had developed among four of these groups—the Germans, the Scandinavians, the Slovaks, and the Greeks. There was also an organization for evangelizing the Armenians.

Though we tend to speak of them as separate entities, such as the Greek Church of God or the German Church of God, this does not imply that they were separate groups but is simply a way of indicating the particular program carried on among and by these people for their own nationality. In order to do this they often set up their own organization and carried on their own publishing work, which was the only logical method, but a basic unity with the total movement continued to exist. The story of the development of the work among each of these national groups is packed with many incidents of daring witness, deep consecration, and sacrificial service.

Among German-Speaking People

There seems to be no record of when the first German-speaking people entered the work of this reformation. The group with which Warner was formerly associated, the Winebrennerian Church of God, had started as a German-speaking communion, and many in that fellowship while Warner was affiliated with it still used German as their principal language. Warner himself could preach in both English and German. Several others of the early leaders could use both languages, so there is little reason to doubt that German-speaking people were among the earliest participants in the movement.

By the early 1890s a sufficient number of German people were involved in the work to create a demand for some literature in that language. In 1892 the editor of the *Gospel Trumpet* began making appeals for money to buy German type and for some consecrated person to learn to set it. The first donation was received in October of that year, and by early 1893 a sufficient amount had come in to buy an "outfit" which could print tracts and books but not a periodical. Even before this type was purchased, the January 5, 1893, issue of the *Gospel Trumpet* had one column in German with English type. On March 23 there were two columns of German, using the newly purchased German type.

About this time also Max DeDerer came to Grand Junction from Louisville, Kentucky, and began translating into German E. E. Byrum's book on divine healing. Within a matter of a few weeks he had also translated about all the tracts then in publication. On February 23, 1893, Warner announced that William Ebel from the West Coast had come to learn the art of typesetting. "In a few days, if God will," the editor wrote, "German tracts will begin to go forth, . . . teaching the way of full salvation."

It was not until January 1, 1895, that a German periodical was issued regularly. This was *Die Evangeliums Posaune* (the *Gospel Trumpet*), edited by Fred L. Hahn and published semimonthly. By 1901 over two thousand copies of each issue were being mailed. Later editors included William Ebel, Dietrich Meyer, Herman G. Babel, Karl Arbeiter, and Gottlieb Arbeiter. In September, 1928, the German publication work was moved to York, Nebraska, and incorporated under the name of Christian Unity Press. The interest in spreading the work among the German-speaking people led to the formation of about thirty congregations, scattered over ten states and four Canadian provinces.

It was from this activity among the German-speaking people in America that the reformation message was carried to Germany and other countries in Europe. The story of the work of such German-American brethren as George Vielguth, William Ebel, Otto Doebert, and Karl Arbeiter in the early part of the twentieth century has already been told, but it should also be mentioned that the German-speaking people in the movement, in both Europe and America, joined together in evangelizing their countrymen in other parts of the world, especially South America. The Solomon Weissburgers and their son Henry and the David Meiers worked faithfully in developing a substantial work among the German-speaking people of Brazil and Argentina as early as 1923.

The American German-speaking work reached a peak in the period just prior to World War I. The vigorous anti-German propaganda of the war years, however, made it difficult to continue to promote this aspect of the movement's outreach. Then too, by this time the second and third generations of the original immigrants were on the scene and there was less interest in preserving the old-world language and customs. In the years that followed, these German language congregations one by one went through the traumatic experience of changing their worship services to English. By the end of World War II there were very few German-speaking congregations of the Church of God in either the United States or Canada.

World events, however, intervened to change the picture again. A new impetus was given to the German work following the close of World War II. Large numbers of displaced persons, largely from East Germany, were relocated in the United States and Canada. Many of these had been associated with the Church of God in Europe and so the German work began over again. This time, though, the situation was different and the problem of relating to the American church was more difficult. The Church of God in Europe had changed less rapidly than in America and the new immigrants were often reluctant to relate to brethren whose life-style as well as language was different than their own, thus extending considerably the cycle of adjustment and amalgamation.

The Scandinavian Work

The spread of the reformation among Scandinavian people began around the turn of the century with the conversion and call to the ministry of several young men from the Danish, Swedish, and Norwegian communities in the north-central section of the United States. Among the earliest of these were O. T. Ring, Thomas Nelson, S. O. Susag, and Olaf Lundy. Later C. J. Forsberg, Nels Renbeck, Otto F. Linn, Lars Olsen, Jens Ikast, and L. P. Peterson figured in the development of the work.

Before any Scandinavian congregations were organized, the leaders began to publish literature for their people. *Den Evangeliiske Basun,* the Dano-Norwegian *Gospel Trumpet,* began publication in Muscatine, Iowa, in February of 1901. Thomas Nelson was the editor of this semimonthly periodical. O. T. Ring, Andrew Welling, and others soon came to assist. In October of that same year the publishing business was moved to a Scandinavian settlement at Grand Forks, North Dakota. The following year, 1902, a suitable property was secured in St. Paul Park, Minnesota, and this became the center of the Scandinavian work for more than twenty years.

In 1903 a Swedish version of the *Gospel Trumpet* was started. O. T. Ring became the editor of the *Evangeli Trumpet* a monthly which was also published at St. Paul Park. In addition to these periodicals many books and tracts were also printed and sent to Scandinavian people in several countries.

By 1909 the Scandinavian congregations in America were sufficiently strong to finance the sending of missionaries to their homelands. O. T. Ring was the first to go. Later Carl J. Forsberg, Nels Renbeck, Morris Johnson, the Ikasts, the Olsens, and others were sent to work in these countries. It was only in its first years, however, that this missionary work was purely a project of the Scandinavian Americans. After the organization of the Missionary Board in Anderson much of this European work was carried on through that agency.

In the meantime St. Paul Park developed into a flourishing Scandinavian center. In one of the buildings on the property which they had purchased they operated an old people's home. It has already been noted that this project was included in the general benevolent program of the church when the Gospel Trumpet Company took it over in 1920. The two periodicals flourished, with the Dano-Norwegian publication becoming a weekly and the Swedish a semimonthly. People from five states gathered at this headquarters for two large conventions each year, and several Scandinavian-speaking congregations were organized.

It is to be observed that the Scandinavian work was always closely allied with the total church, so in 1923, when it seemed advisable to concentrate on the missionary aspect of the Scandinavian-language project, the St. Paul Park interests were moved to Denmark and Sweden under the general supervision of the Missionary Board. The Scandinavian groups in the United States eventually changed their services to English and found their place in the ongoing life of the church.

The Slovak Brethren

Another significant intercultural development in the movement was among the Slovak people in eastern Ohio, western Pennsylvania, and Connecticut. This work began in Sharon, Pennsylvania, in 1905 when Samuel Fabry became interested in a tent meeting being held in that city by J. Grant Anderson and H. M. Riggle. Fabry, along with several other Slovakians, had been won to the Winebrennerian Church of God about three years before, and at the time of the tent meeting were worshiping with that group in Sharon. After hearing the reformation message he severed his relations with the Winebrennerians and began holding meetings in the homes of his friends. The result was the first Slovak congregation of the Church of God.

Two other ministers, John Cerbus and John Horevay, were soon assisting Fabry in spreading the message among these people. In addition to Anderson and Riggle, several other English-speaking ministers, such as I. S. McCoy, C. M. Boyer, G. H. Pye, and John L. Williams preached to the Slovak people through interpreters. The net result of these efforts was the establishment of several congregations which conducted their services in the Slovenian tongue. Horevay was responsible for getting churches started in New Kensington, Johnstown, and Smithfield, Pennsylvania, and in Campbell, Ohio. Fabry launched a congregation in Torrington, Connecticut and later went to Akron, Ohio and started a new church there. Cerbus took over the work in Sharon. While pastor here he also preached in Butler and Arnold, Pennsylvania.

The Slovak people began to develop their own literature in the early 1920s under the leadership of Michael Fabry, son of Samuel Fabry. A press was purchased and set up in the church basement in Akron. Many tracts were translated and printed. The two major publication projects were a hymnbook, *Melodie Sionske,* published in 1929, and a monthly periodical, the *Hlasnik* (Herald), which was started in 1930. Michael Fabry died in 1935, but the publishing work was continued by the elder Fabry until his death in 1944. It was then that Paul Yanik, Jr., became the editor. Under his leadership the publication activity was stepped up considerably. New printing equipment was purchased and distribution of the periodical was extended to Slovak people in South America, Africa, and several countries in eastern Europe. At one time there were almost 2,000 subscribers in Czechoslovakia alone. The "iron curtain" closed this opportunity completely, however, and the increasing use of English by Slovak Americans reduced the demand at home, and so all Slovak publications were discontinued in 1958.

In 1926 the Slovak people purchased a tract of land near Hubbard, Ohio and developed a facility for conducting an annual camp meeting. Until the 1940s all services were in the Slovak language. Gradually more and more of the meetings were in English. By 1970 Slovak was no longer used in any of the general meetings. The campground then came to be used by all the Church of God congregations in that area. By this time all of the Slovak congregations also had changed the language of their worship services to English, so the era of an ethnic Slavic work in the Church of God in America came to an end.

There was, however, a very significant continuing ministry in the Slovak Language. In 1948 Paul Yanik, Jr., began producing a taped radio program called "Slovak Church of the Air." It came to be broadcast on five stations in Ohio and Pennsylvania. This outreach ministry continued for ten years until Yanik left his pastorate and moved to Anderson, Indiana, to prepare himself to go to Czechoslovakia as a missionary. Political events and health problems prevented him from realizing this objective, but he never lost his dream of evangelizing the people of the land from which his ancestors came. Radio seemed to be the only open door for doing this, and so, while working as a printer at Warner Press he purchased the necessary equipment and built a studio in his home. In 1971 an audition tape was accepted for broadcast by Trans World Radio, the 100,000 watt short wave station in Monte Carlo, Monaco. Since then Yanik's fifteen-minute Slovak program, "Living Waters," has been broadcast weekly and beamed to cover all of east Europe. Costs are covered largely by contributions.

The Greek Work

The work of the reformation among the Greeks in America

really had it beginnings in Egypt. It was there in 1915 that Constantine (Gus) Nicholaou was converted under the ministry of G. K. Ouzounian. The following year he came to America and began preaching among his countrymen in Salt Lake City, Utah. Three years later he and two of his converts went to Anderson Bible Training School. After spending a year in study he and his friends went again into evangelistic work among their own people. Among these early workers were Constantine Stavropoulos, Sam Lellos, Michael Stergiou, Nick Zazanis, and Nick Stergiou. The latter two began publishing a Greek version of the *Gospel Trumpet* around 1920 while they were students in Anderson Bible Training School. The following year Zazanis went to Chicago and took the publishing work with him.

As the result of efforts by these men and others such as George Dallas, Bill Conkis, Chris Angelos, Athanasius Chionos, Anestes Karamitros, and John Pappas, Greek-speaking congregations were developed in perhaps a dozen or more cities in the United States and extensive missionary effort was directed to Egypt and Greece. The work of the Church of God in Athens, for instance, was the result of evangelistic work by Zazanis Lellos, and Chionos, with Zazanis remaining to serve as pastor for many years. In 1946 this Athens congregation received official recognition by the Greek government. A new strategically located and beautifully designed building was dedicated in 1955. Through the years the Church of God in Greece has maintained a close relationship with the Greek churches in America and with the Missionary Board, which has assisted in funding and supplying leadership.

By the late 1960s the number of Greek-speaking congregations in the United States had dwindled to three—those in Detroit, Chicago, and Gary, Indiana. The pattern of change was different, however, among the Greeks than for other ethnic groups. Instead of changing the language and remaining in the same setting, they merged with neighboring English-speaking congregations. In 1969 the (Greek) Belmont church in Chicago joined with the Northwest Church of God. In 1971 the Greek church in Detroit merged with the Northwestern congregation to become the Farmington Hills Church of God and the Greek pastor, John Pappas, became a copastor of the newly formed group. The following year, 1972, the Greek church in Gary joined forces with the congregation in Schererville, Indiana. The Greek publishing work in Chicago discontinued operation in 1971.

Points for Discussion

1. What particular conditions in America made it possible for the work of the Church of God to spread to several cultural groups?
2. Briefly sketch the beginning of the work among the various foreign-language groups discussed in this chapter.
3. The 1919 *Yearbook* of the Church of God listed the languages each minister could speak. Would this be a good feature today?
4. Is it inevitable that foreign-language churches should eventually change over to the prevailing language of the country? Under what conditions can such groups continue to grow?
5. What are the implications of the new interest in desegregation of black and white people for prevailing practices in the Church of God?
6. In what specific ways has the Church of God made progress in transcending color barriers? What steps might be taken to make the movement's teaching on Christian unity more meaningful in regard to race relations?

CHAPTER XI

THE PROGRESS OF THE MOVEMENT

The preceding chapters have attempted to look back rather carefully over the road which the Church of God reformation movement has traveled. There is good reason now to turn from this backward view and focus attention on the present place to which this road from the past has led. With almost a century of history behind it, where does the movement now stand in relation to its own past and to the whole of Christianity? What indications are there that the real goals of the reformation are being accomplished? Have there been significant changes in viewpoint and attitude within the movement? Is there evidence that genuine progress has been made?

A complete answer to these questions would, of course, require a full-scale analysis of every portion of the church's development, and even then the picture would be incomplete, for there are many intangible aspects of a movement such as this in which progress is not measurable in concrete terms. Even so, it is possible to make certain comparisons with the past, to mark some of the significant mileposts of development, and to note a few of the changes. These comparisons will perhaps help to make clear, at least partially, the significance of what has happened and will enable one to appraise a little more intelligently the state of the movement in terms of its total relationships.

Growth

The most obvious way to judge the progress of a movement, of course, is to note the growth in the number of people who are affiliated with it. Such a statistical study, which would be relatively simple for most groups, becomes a major problem, however, for the Church of God reformation. No accurate figures are available. The principle first set forth by the pioneers that God alone has the right to determine who is a member of the church has been followed through the years. The congregations do not "take in" members, and no official rolls are kept. In order to get an estimate of size each group is asked to report the number of persons who appear to be members; that is, those who regularly attend services and testify to a personal experience of redemption through Christ. The movement had been in existence more than forty years before even this loose way of estimating membership came into use, so there are no early records available. Only since 1923 has any tabulation been kept indicating the numerical size of the movement.

A review of this record reveals that the growth of the movement has been steady. At the beginning of 1925, after almost four and one-half decades of existence, a total of almost 27,000 members in 685 congregations was reported. The next ten-year period, however, saw a gain which could be described as almost phenomenal. The 1935 total in 1,352 congregations is listed at just under 60,000, an increase of 122 percent. Another decade later, 1945, the number of listed members had grown to almost 90,000, and by 1955 the total membership figure for the 2,141 congregations in the United States and Canada was nearly 122,000. The next decade saw an increase to 143,000 and by 1975 the reported total membership in 2,284 congregations had reached 164,000. To use these figures as a measure of size comparable with other church groups is, of course, misleading. This is well illustrated by the fact that for 1975 the reported average Sunday morning attendance totaled over 310,000, which is only slightly less than double the membership estimate for that year.

Another measure of numerical strength is Sunday school enrollment. This is perhaps a more accurate figure since it is based on actual class rolls. Despite the relatively slow start for Sunday schools in the movement, enrollment by 1925 totaled more than 49,000. By 1935 this figure had climbed substantially to 87,000. Then, during the decade of the "1,000 new Sunday schools" campaign, enrollment jumped to 144,000. The next ten years saw an even greater numerical increase with enrollment reaching 216,000 by 1955. The rate of increase slowed somewhat but the total in 1965 was up to 252,000. The decade ending 1975 brought a leveling off and even a slight decrease to 244,000 persons enrolled in Sunday schools in the United States and Canada.

These figures, however, tell only a portion of the story, for by 1975 the Church of God was at work in a total of 53 countries of the world. Accurate statistics for membership outside the United States and Canada are difficult to obtain since there is no central reporting system. A calculated estimate would put the number at approximately 99,000. When this is added to the 1975 domestic membership figure of 164,000 this would bring the world-wide membership total to approximately 263,000. If Sunday attendance reports from other countries were available to add to the 310,000 at home it is likely that the total 1975 constituency of the movement would approach the half-million mark.

Standing alone, these figures may seem somewhat imposing, but in comparison with other religious bodies in the world they do not indicate that this reformation movement is yet taking over the rest of Christianity. Some American denominations report a membership of thirteen million and more, so the Church of God still cannot be classed as one of the major religious bodies of America or of the world. Even so, the size of the movement and its rate of growth indicate a vitality and an appeal far above what would be considered ordinary. As a point of comparison it may be noted that in the fifty-year period between 1925 and 1975 the population of the United States almost doubled and the membership of the Church of God increased by more than sixfold.

Acquisitions

Another common method of measuring progress is in terms of what the group owns. While it must be borne in mind that the valuation of property holdings has little to do with the real worth of a movement and that such figures, even when available, are difficult to analyze, it still must be recognized that statistics in this area can reveal a great deal about the character of a group. In the thirty-year period, 1925-1955, the valuation of property owned by the church as a whole (colleges and national agency holdings) increased by almost three million dollars—from $750,000 in 1925 to $3,741,000 in 1955. The next twenty years, however, saw this figure multiplied more than seven times to a total of $26,832,000 in 1975. On a per capita basis this means that in 1925 each member of the Church of God had $27.84 invested in national property. After thirty years there had been only a $4.10 increase to $31.94 per person. Another twenty years later, however, the per capita investment at this level had reached $164.77.

Of even greater significance from the standpoint of what is really happening in the Church of God are the reports of the valuation of local church property. In 1925 local congregations owned property valued at around $2,500,000. In thirty years (by 1955) this had increased to $43,476,530, and by 1975 the total valuation had reached $200,376,700. Translated into per capita investment this means that in the thirty-year span between 1925 and 1955 the increase was from $81.73 to $371.12 per person. In the next twenty years the figure jumped to $1,813.27 for 1975, over 22 times the per capita local investment a half century earlier.

These figures could be used to prove a number of things—some good and some not so good. In a very real way they tell their own story. They say a great deal about priorities, programs, and people. At the national level they speak of expanding colleges and a growing seminary, of an enlarging publishing work, of program agencies whose swelling work-load demands more office space and better equipment, of a new auditorium for an increasingly significant international convention, and of the constant concern to function more efficiently and improve working conditions. Woven into these statistics is the graphic design of a movement demanding more space and better facilities to carry on its enlarging ministry.

At the local level these statistics speak of much that is routine but more that is dramatic. They tell of persons with dreams but often with little except a deep commitment to make those dreams come true. They repeat over and over again the story of faithful people brought together in a particular place by their shared vision of "the Church," sacrificing every penny they could spare, and some they could not spare, in order to get a church building of their own, even if it were no more than an old store building or a remodeled house. There is also the story of struggle after struggle to move churches to better locations.

These figures also tell of changing tastes in architecture and a growing awareness of the beautiful. Where once a tabernacle type structure, often built of secondhand lumber, was considered an adequate place of worship, the time has come when more and more congregations are planning their new church buildings with the help of a trained architect. The greater concern for beauty has made the traditional types of church architecture with stained-glass windows, pipe organs, and laminated arches more common in the small sanctuaries as well as in the larger churches.

Beyond this, these figures on increasing property values tell the story of Sunday school facilities crowded beyond capacity, of classes meeting in nearby homes, in school busses, and under trees. They tell of building additions and remodeling programs which were often too small by the time they were finished. They tell of the increasing demands of growing youth groups, of additional space needed for boys' and girls' clubs, vacation church school, and day nurseries. They tell of a movement with a vigorous program and a widened ministry which demands more and more facilities to keep it going. Behind the cold dollar signs are warmhearted, dedicated people who are willing to give more and do more that the kingdom may be extended.

Giving

Expansion, improvement, and growth of the church at any

level is not possible unless there is a vision of what needs to be done, a strategy to accomplish the goals which are set, and enthusiasm for the "cause" which has been defined. At almost every point along the path of progress, money is a key factor. If dreams are to be actualized and if plans are to become reality there must be sufficient funds. In the church, funds are generally available only to the extent that members contribute, so in assessing the progress of the movement it becomes important to review the giving pattern of people in congregations of the Church of God.

Here again, early records are unavailable. There was not what could be considered a national fund raising effort until the late 1920s when the "Associated Budgets" program became operative. By 1935 the combined budgets for the general agencies totaled $150,000. A decade later the goal had increased to $250,000, but, in the wake of the previous year's "Quarter Million Campaign," a total of $386,000, or $4.37 per captia, was actually raised. In 1955 giving to the general causes had tripled to a total of $1,109,428 and the per capita figure had risen to $11.26. In another ten years the total was over half a million dollars higher at $1,650,011, but the per capita figure remained about the same. By 1975 the World Service budget had more than doubled the figure of a decade earlier and had risen to $3,427,500. Per capita giving reached a record high of $22.00 in order to achieve this.

These figures tell only a small portion of the story for they report only giving to the general causes, and this represents about seven percent of the total amount donated to the church. When contributions to local congregations, to state and district work, and to other projects are added it would multiply each of the above figures by fourteen. This would mean, for instance, that total giving for 1975 would be approximately $48 million, which is almost $300.00 per capita.

Lest any of this discussion of the total economic growth of the movement give the impression that all the congregations of the Church of God are affluent, well staffed, and have beautiful sanctuaries in prosperous neighborhoods, it would be well, perhaps, to note another fact or two which highlight a major problem—small congregations. Half of the congregations in the movement have fifty or fewer members. Only twenty-two percent have a membership of 100 or more. The average size of a congregation in 1975 was seventy-two. This means that most churches are still struggling with the basics of survival—leadership and facilities. There is often inadequate support for a pastor as well as an unsuitable place of worship. Thus, even though the total figures on acquisitions and giving may be significantly large, the predominance of weak congregations often forces a preoccupation with bare maintenance and a "making do" with limited leadership. This condition, it must be said also, provides some tremendous examples of sacrificial giving and dedicated living.

Structure

It is only natural that the passing of time and growth in size of the movement should bring modifications in structure. The early antipathy to organization and the subsequent development of such agencies as seemed necessary to carry on the cooperative work of the group have already been noted. For the most part any changes in the structure have sought to preserve the basic principle of governance by the Holy Spirit and have continued the essential elements of the national pattern established in 1917 with the creation of the General Assembly and the several subordinate boards related to it. In reviewing the developments in organization since that time at least three processes, unarticulated and largely unconscious, seem to have been in operation.

The first of these processes may be described as *deputizing*. This is the general philosophy that changes should be made only when a need arises or a problem emerges; then a person or corporate group should be designated to deal with it. The result is that many changes in procedure have been made on the basis of expediency or necessity rather than according to a preconceived plan. For example, when congregations began to object to separate promotional bombardment by each of the general agencies a cooperative plan was developed in 1927. The Associated Budgets Committee functioned until 1941 when the World Service Commission was formed. Further refinements in this structure were made in 1955 when the Executive Council was reorganized and its Division of World Service became responsible for this fund raising and promotional activity. In each case changes were made to correct inadequacies in the previous arrangement.

Another example would be youth work. When the young people of the church began to seek more meaningful involvement in the 1930s they began a process which went through several stages of improvement—a study committee, a separate organization, and eventually integration into the program of the Board of Christian Education. Other deeply felt concerns found their way into structural expression in varying ways. Women's work and men's work emerged as independent national organizations. Minister's pensions became a board under the General Assembly. Radio and television, higher education, social concerns, and Christian unity became Commissions under the Executive Council. Other issues have been handled by committees, task forces, caucuses, and other groups deputized to take care of an area of concern.

The second process which has been operative is that of *democratizing*. Almost all of the organizational changes since 1917 point toward an increasing spiritual democracy throughout the whole church. Despite the strong objection to "man rule" in the early days, the first fifty years of the movement's history saw no period when several big-name leaders did not dominate the scene, either on a sectional or a national scale. Such domination was not intentional, perhaps, and almost without exception was because of the recognized ability of the person rather than because he held any office which gave him authority. Even so, today in the place of the big names, committees, boards, and other democratically chosen groups make the decisions and determine policies for the movement.

Examples of this trend are legion. Notable among the democratizing developments are: opening the General Assembly to lay people who are members of a national agency, eliminating multiple membership on more than one board or the Executive Council, prohibiting staff or employees of one agency serving on the board of other agencies, inviting state organizations to send observers to meetings of the Executive Council, giving special attention to including minority groups and women as members and staff, and limitation on the number of terms a person may serve on the Executive Council and some of the general boards. All of these changes are in the direction of involving more people in places of responsibility and influence in the movement.

The third process in structural development which has been prominently evident is that of *decentralizing*. Although a great deal of programing and promotion comes from national offices in Anderson, Indiana, a growing amount of both of these functions is being done at other levels. Some of the national agencies, particularly in the areas of Christian education, church extension, and evangelism, have fostered deliberately the creation of state or regional units to implement the causes which they represent. Two of the national agencies, both colleges, operate in their own locations outside Anderson.

Perhaps one of the most significant aspects of the structural development of the movement has been the growth of state and district organization. Organization on a regional basis began almost as early as organization at the national level, but only since the early 1930s have state assemblies come to play a really significant role in the total work of the church. The beginning of prominence was probably when these organizations were asked to ratify those ministers from their district whose names should appear in the *Yearbook*. The status of these sectional ratification committees was further raised when C. E. Brown, after becoming editor of the *Gospel Trumpet* in 1930, announced that he would depend on the judgment of these committees in determining whose articles and reports would be considered for publication.

With the development of state camp meetings, state conventions of various types, and eventually state projects in evangelism, the need for funds at this level became apparent, so many states began to set up their own promotional programs and to employ state workers for administering and coordinating their expanding functions. By 1975 fourteen state organizations had secured at least one employed staff person to implement their programs. Of even greater significance than this development itself is the fact that most states have established associational type structures which include lay delegates from the congregations as well as ministers.

The net result of all these developments is a polity which cannot be described by any of the traditional labels applied to church governmental systems. In a very real sense the movement functions congregationally, for each local congregation is autonomous, owns its own property, calls its own pastor, and is subject to no quotas or assessments. In another sense a great deal of the cooperative work of the church, especially at the state level, operates in a presbyterian manner through delegated groups who function on behalf of those who select them. In still another sense the episcopal pattern has been prominent despite the absense of bishops, for until relatively recent times the clergy has been responsible for most of the decision making. The important point, of course, is not whether a particular system is followed but whether procedures are always open to direction and guidance by the Holy Spirit.

Doctrines

The Church of God reformation began with an "open-at-the-top" view of religious truth. The highest compliment which could be paid to the present leadership would be to say that this is still the case. In general this is true, although it needs to be said that on at least a few occasions there have been strong tendencies toward putting on the lid and saying, "Now we have it all, and no more will be accepted." One of the reasons for this inclination, perhaps, is that consolidation was taking place in other ways, and so it was only natural that "truth" should come to be defined once and for all. Another contributing factor was the fact that certain leaders came to be looked upon as "specialists" in specific doctrines, and what those persons said was often considered the final word. Everyone in the movement during the twenties and thirties knew that E. E. Byrum was the chief spokesman on divine healing, that H. M. Riggle was the authority on the second coming of Christ, and that F. G. Smith was the foremost interpreter of the Book of Revelation. All of them, along with many others, were also well versed on the doctrine of the church.

The passing of this period of the specialists seemed at first to leave a great doctrinal void, but it soon became apparent that with third- and fourth-generation people making up the bulk of the movement the "old truths" must once again be stated in contemporary language so that the present generation may discover anew the thrill of the message which sent the pioneers out as "flying messengers." Such motivation is rarely achieved with a second- or third-hand message. On the whole, it may be said that the movement is now more aware of the necessity of a sound basis of belief than it has ever been. Very few of the younger generation, however, are willing to accept their faith in neat little doses from the past. They want to search the Scriptures anew and find the foundation for a broad base of belief which will comprehend not only the doctrines emphasized by the pioneers but also everything else that is vital to Christianity.

Such a process inevitably brings certain modifications in emphasis. Most of these changes are either in method or in vocabulary and not in basic truth, for truth itself does not change. There are many roads which lead to the same destination, and simply because one has not traveled the same road as another does not mean that he has not arrived. Likewise, there are many words which might describe a glorious sight, and simply because one does not use the same words as another does not mean that he does not behold the beauty which surrounds him.

An examination of the Sunday school curriculum materials, of articles in *Vital Christianity,* of the books and pamphlets which are published, and of the sermons which are preached from Sunday to Sunday would reveal that sound biblical doctrine in its broadest sense is as much of a concern in the movement at the present time as it has ever been in the past.

Points for Discussion

1. How may the progress of a movement be judged?
2. Can an increase in numbers always be considered growth? Explain and illustrate.
3. Why is material gain a deceptive measure of progress? What are some of the factors behind the growth in property valuation in the Church of God?
4. Name some of the organizational developments which have helped the movement do a better job of ministering to people. Have these developments been consistent with the principle of rule by the Holy Spirit?
5. Explain how statements of belief may change but truth never changes.

CHAPTER XII

THE ROAD AHEAD

This historical study of the Church of God reformation would not be complete without a serious consideration of the probable future developments in the movement. It is impossible, of course, to predict with certainty what is going to happen, even in the next instant, but with a survey of the movement's past fresh in mind and a knowledge of the present close at hand, it is possible to note the general direction in which the movement is going and to foresee some of the likely outcomes to present trends. Though not yet known, that which lies ahead is already in the process of being made. In the final analysis, the future of any enterprise is largely a projection of its past, and subsequent developments are usually the fruition of plans which have been laid long before.

With this approach in mind it becomes profitable, then, to ask a few searching questions about what is now "in the works" as far as the Church of God is concerned. These questions should highlight some of the factors which will help to determine the future development of the movement.

What Are the Long-Range Goals?

One of the first observations which needs to be made is that the movement is likely to become what it intends to become. Whatever goals the group sets for itself will in large measure determine its character and its success. A great deal of the genius of the early leaders was the sharpness of their objectives and the forthright manner in which they moved toward realizing them.

The objectives defined by the pioneers, however, had been formulated by a few of the central leaders who, in an unofficial but nevertheless authoritative sense, spoke for the whole group. Others who identified with the movement did so because they accepted, at least in a broad sense, these already defined goals. As the years passed and the group increased in size there was a corresponding increase in the demand for wider involvement in the processes of assessing programs and defining objectives. The result, as already noted, was a continuing trend toward democratizing procedures, but along with this there seems to have been a tendency toward accepting more generalized goals. By the end of the 1930s many were daring to ask questions about "reason for being " and "where are we going?"

This created a period of uneasiness which prompted a veritable avalanche of analysis. A great deal of this took place in informal discussion, but there was much that was deliberate and scholarly. In a period of two decades beginning around 1940 there were over a dozen graduate theses, at least three doctoral dissertations, and a number of books and pamphlets which turned on the searchlight of self-analysis. The movement was examined theologically, historically, and sociologically. Put together, these studies contributed considerably to a clearer self-understanding and pointed up the need for sharpening a sense of definite direction and purpose for the movement.

Leaders apparently read the signs well. In slightly more than one decade there were no less than four major opportunities for overall assessment of the movement and goal-setting for the future. The first of these large-scale introspective exercises took the form of an "All Board Congress" in October, 1963. The 260 participants—members and staff of all national boards, state coordinators, and one representative from each state—met for three days to clarify issues and identify goals. After an "agonizing reappraisal" they defined sixteen "needs" and set forth five "overarching concerns."

The second opportunity for assessment came seven years later with the calling of another church-wide conference designated as the "1970 Consultation of the Church of God." Seeking to build upon the previous Congress this meeting's purpose was to "find clear direction for the Church in the 1970s." After extensive advance preparation, which included six "projection" papers, responses, and reading suggestions, the 170 participants met for four days with the major portion of the time spent in six "area" work groups. Findings in each of these areas was summarized.

The third opportunity followed very quickly, for in June of that same year the General Assembly acted favorably on a resolution calling for a "Consultation on Doctrine," the purpose of which would be "to restudy the theological and doctrinal message of our movement." Instead of a single consultation this turned out to be a series of thirty meetings conducted over a three year period, mostly in regularly scheduled state assemblies, with approximately 2,200 persons involved. Findings were summarized for the 1974 General Assembly in a thirty-six page booklet.

The fourth exercise in goal setting, much less extensive in scope, came in the spring of 1974 when a group of twenty-five persons—eighteen members of the Division of General Service and seven state coordinators—met for two days at Yokefellow House in Richmond, Indiana, and drew up a two and one-half page "Yokefellow Statement" of objectives for the movement in the "immediate years leading up to our Centennial Celebration."

Drawing upon the documents produced by these four conferences, an attempt will be made to set forth projections for the road ahead in several areas.

Identity

Perhaps the most important question any religious group can ask itself is, "What are we about?" The Church of God has dared to face this question, and the answers have not always been precise enough to be entirely satisfactory. The crisis phase of the identity problem of the 1940s passed, but the imperative continually to maintain a clear sense of purpose is ever present. The 1963 Congress spoke of the need to know "*who* we are and *why* we are." The Yokefellow Statement hit the issue head-on by naming "identity" as the area of first concern and declaring,

"We affirm the reformational role of the Church of God movement," and then the statement goes on to speak of a commitment to "nourish those things that draw us together."

For the "come-outers" of the late nineteenth century, reason for being was no problem. The great motivation behind the "flying messengers" of pioneer days was that they had a positive ultimate goal in mind. They were reformers, but their objective was not just the removal of a few unwholesome conditions which had developed in the Christian church. They sought to tear away the whole structure of the sectarian system, to restore the church to its original foundations, and to reconstitute it in unity and holiness. Their methods may sometimes have been crude, but their message was vital. They were dynamic because they had some ultimates toward which they were striving.

In a general sense *raison d'etre* defined by the pioneers should continue to be the purpose of the movement until that objective, the one holy church, is achieved. But for each succeeding generation this goal needs to be redefined and restated so that it will be meaningful in contemporary terms. Today's and tomorrow's participants in the reformation movement must be just as convinced that the movement has a reason for existence as were the first promoters of the reform. Without ultimate purpose what was once a dynamic movement becomes only a comfortable institution.

Doctrine

One of the most consistently articulated concerns is that of continuing faithfulness to a solid core of biblical truth. The movement has never been creedal but it has been intensely doctrinal. The All Board Congress headed its list with "the need for clearer, stronger theological foundations." The "biblical and theological imperative" was affirmed as the first focal point for setting objectives in the opening address of the 1970 Consultation. The whole purpose, of course, of the 1971-74 series of consultations was doctrinal clarification. The

Yokefellow Statement called upon the church to "restore the biblical root system of our heritage."

The crucial issue, of course, in any reemphasis on doctrine is to determine how precise the definitions should be. There are those who would want to draw up a set of specific declarations and make them a test of fellowship; others fear the specter of creedalism and defend the historic stance of openness. All the consultations frankly faced the fact of divergent doctrinal positions in the movement and noted polarizations which possibly could lead even to schism. There was little inclination, however, to formulate a creed and demand rigid adherence. Christian unity is rooted deeper than doctrinal agreement at every point. The road ahead theologically seems to be: keep biblical, keep flexible, keep seeking truth, keep as close together as possible, and keep variant understandings from undermining unity.

Structure

Each of the assessment meetings referred to dealt very specifically with issues related to polity. Because of the movement's historic aversion to organization, based on the valid premise that the church is God's and not man's, there has been a reluctance to give any more attention than absolutely necessary to structure. Through the years, however, there has been a growing realization that if a group is to function corporately there must be certain understood procedures. More recently there has been the additional insight that the *way* a group functions has a great deal to do with what it accomplishes. Consequently, participants in these consultations raised questions about such matters as a delegated general assembly (recognizing that many state organizations have already moved in this direction), a more representatively structured Executive Council, and other points at which a greater degree of participatory democracy at every level of church organization could be achieved.

As a group becomes larger its structure becomes more

complex. The more complex the structure, the more rigid it tends to become. In the past the Church of God movement has been able to keep its organizational framework fairly flexible, but the question is whether it can continue to keep it so with the addition of more controls at the local, state, and national levels. Does the creation of more boards and committees with executive and judicial powers create any hazard to future development?

The real question involved here, of course, is not whether such organizations are legitimate and necessary, for any democratically structured group requires such agents to plan and carry out various aspects of the work. A very critical point for the future of the movement, though, is whether there will be a constant awareness that the multiplication of organization tends to make the structure more rigid and to limit the free operation of the Holy Spirit. The pioneers were right in noting this tendency, and it must not be forgotten, regardless of how complex the structure may become. The danger lies not so much in the organization itself but in forgetting that this organization is but a vehicle for carrying out the will of the Holy Spirit.

Church Growth

Another of the repeatedly expressed concerns has been that the movement would more adequately implement the real mission of the church. Denoted variously as evangelism, missions, church renewal, and communicating the gospel, the desired objective is the upbuilding and extension of the church in the world. The All Board Congress expressed its concerns in this area by expressing five needs, out of the sixteen they identified, in this category, using such terms as spiritual renewal, vital evangelism, better communication, redemptive fellowship, and the whole church's ministry. The 1970 Consultation gave massive attention to church growth in that four of the six study areas were devoted to this concern: lay ministry, evangelism, missions, and leadership. The doctrinal consultations on the church devoted one-fourth of its attention to "the mission of the church," and the Yokefellow Statement expressed similar concerns under the heading of "ministry."

Taken as a whole it may be noted that this is not a neglected area of concern. All of the church's program boards are giving constant attention to improvement and expansion, whether it be Sunday schools, church extension, or overseas missions. The church's educational institutions gear their curricula to preparing both clergy and lay leaders for ministry and witness. State organizations and local congregations are growth oriented and constantly clamor for new tools and know-how to help them do it faster and better.

Despite all this attention, the growth of the Church of God, as already noted, has not been phenomenal. So the road ahead is a demanding one—demanding more productivity, plus added resources; more witnesses, highly motivated and better trained; more money, used more judiciously; more effort, expended where needs are greatest; more planning and coordination, preventing duplication and waste; more expectation, tackling the really big jobs; more faith, letting God help; and more consecration, partnering with the Holy Spirit.

Social Concerns

The 1963 Congress identified a need for a "heightened social conscience and consciousness," and confessed "our need for guidance in the proper expression of social concerns." The 1970 Consultation had "social concerns" as the first of its six areas of study and the keynote speaker observed, "We are only moderately involved in civic and social work. . . . We do, however, have a bad conscience about this." In the consultation itself social issues came to the fore in almost every other section, particularly questions relating to implications of the gospel regarding race. A great deal of attention was given to practices within the movement itself which might have racist implications. In discussions on the nature of the church in the doctrinal consultations social concerns were not specifically on the agenda, but they emerged repeatedly in dealing with the issues of unity and mission. The Yokefellow Statement devoted almost one-fourth of its text to the matter of "integration," noting that "the church must continuously work its way through and beyond racial relationships to functional unity."

The creation of the Commission on Social Concerns in 1964 provided a vehicle for calling attention to needs but did not create an instrument for serving needs. The Commission was not set up as a programming agency; it was authorized to speak *to* the church but not *for* the church. It may lift up issues and encourage other agencies to act along recommended lines. Various of the church's agencies have acted, and in significant ways.

The fact of the matter is that the Church of God movement is not yet adequately structured for an ongoing program of Christian social action. The concerns are conscious, but the strategies are undefined and unimplemented. The road ahead is open but uncharted, and no one is responsible for drawing a map.

Christian Unity

Without question the area where almost all participants in the movement feel their deepest concern and express their greatest hope is in regard to the unity of the church. From the beginning to the present there has been this vision of overcoming sectarian division and realizing the answer to Christ's prayer that all his followers be one. Many statements in all the consultations reflect this dream. The continuing question, of course, is how this may come about and particularly how this movement relates to the rest of Christianity.

There is no denying that the future of the Church of God movement is dependent to a great extent on what happens in all of Christianity. The movement must take either a positive or a negative response to whatever general developments take place. In the early days the response was mostly negative. As already noted the message of unity met considerable opposition, for the reformers were almost alone in such an emphasis. Because the lines were rather sharply drawn it was considered compromise to cooperate with the sects in any way.

In the years since the founding of the movement, however, conditions have changed considerably. Many of the same groups who formerly strongly opposed the "radical" message of unity have now become stanch advocates of the doctrine. Everywhere there is evidence of striving to bring about better relations between Christians in different denominational groups. The religious climate in regard to this doctrine has changed almost completely.

This raises some interesting questions about the relation of the Church of God to these other Christian groups. Will the movement lose the distinctiveness of its message if it joins in certain cooperative ventures with friendly denominations? Will participation in agencies such as the World Council of Churches mean settling for "union" instead of "unity"? Does the Church of God have anything to contribute in the world-wide quest to find a solution to the problem of Christian disunity? If so, through what channels can this contribution be made?

The answers to these questions are crucial to the whole future of Christianity as well as to the future of the Church of God movement. It needs to be recognized that great strides have been made since the turn of the twentieth century in regard to Christian unity, but the Church of God has had very little to do with any of them because of its policy of nonparticipation. The nature of the developments up to this time do not seem to raise serious questions about the wisdom of the movement's policy, for there was probably an unreadiness on the part of others to consider seriously what leaders in this movement would have to say. But what about the future?

The ecumenical agencies make no claim to having arrived at a final answer. After studying differences and likenesses for almost half a century ecumenical leaders seem to be searching for direction in regard to what should be the next steps along the road toward unity. Is it at this point that the teachings of the Church of God on this subject may be pertinent? Is the Christian world now more ready for the viewpoints for which this group has stood than at earlier times in the history of the movement? The answer to both these questions seems to be yes.

This, then, is no time to be soft-pedaling the message. It is time to proclaim it with renewed vigor and in the places where it will do the most good. The future of the Church of God is closely related to its witness to the truth that people are united in spirit only as they are united in Christ, and that true visible unity can be achieved as all participate in the common experience of redemption and submit to the divine leadership of the Holy Spirit.

Open To All Truth

The last and more important question to be asked is whether or not the Church of God reformation will remain faithful to the principle set forth by the pioneers that truth is ever-advancing. In promoting and defending what they believed to be "the truth," these early leaders were not particularly distinctive. Almost every religious group has made a similar claim. But where others said, "This is it!" and built a wall around their particular insights, these people boldly asserted the truth of their own revelation and then quickly added, "There is more to come."

The implications of this concept are tremendous. It means that there must be a constant striving for more knowledge and new insights. It means that the movement must be always pushing ahead and thrusting back its frontiers. To continue to wrestle with dead issues of days gone by can result only in a stagnation of message and a rejection of progress. To be a dynamic force in the world the movement must be continually alert to contemporary needs and be willing to adapt to changes in the religious climate both in local communities and in the world at large. While seeking to preserve all the values of the past, the prevailing mood of the group must be that of eagerness to reform itself so that it may ever keep on the growing edge of every aspect of truth.

To sum it all up, what happens to the Church of God reformation in the future will depend in large part on how faithful succeeding generations are to the principle held by the pioneers that truth as understood by finite man is never static. It continues to move ahead. Our understanding can never quite comprehend it in its entirety, but we must continue the pursuit. The big question for the Church of God, then, is whether or not it will be able to keep abreast of the spirit of truth as it marches down the road ahead.

Points for Discussion

1. What is the real reason for the existence of the Church of God reformation movement? What purposes and goals does your own congregation have that could not be accomplished by some other Christian group?
2. In what ways is your church's program geared to the real needs of people?
3. What are some of the changes in world Christianity which have taken place since the beginning of this movement?
4. In what sense is this movement still a reformation?
5. What are some of the implications of the open-ended view of truth held by the pioneers in the Church of God reformation movement?

APPENDIX

Since A Brief History of the Church of God *was written in 1976, there has been considerable change in the structure of the national agencies of the Church of God and in the names of various institutions. This appendix provides the current name and status of many of these entities.*

Anderson University
Started as the Anderson Bible Training School, Anderson College became Anderson University in 1987.

Board of Church Extension
In 2003, the Board of Church Extension entered into a court-ordered dissolution.

Christians Broadcasting Hope
In 1953, the Radio and Television Commission was created to oversee the national Church of God radio program, the *Christian Brotherhood Hour*. In 1976, the Radio and Television Commission became the Mass Communications Board of the Church of God. In the mid-1990s, the *Christian Brotherhood Hour* became *Christians Broadcasting Hope*. Today, Christians Broadcasting Hope refers to the worldwide radio ministries of the Church of God; the English program is now called *ViewPoint*. The Mass Communications Board of the Church of God has become CBH/ Mass Media, a department of Church of God Ministries (see entry).

Church of God Ministries, Inc.
In 1997, the General Assembly approved a plan to reorganize the structure of the national agencies. Implementation was completed in December 1999. Today, Church of God Ministries, Inc., continues the ministries previously assigned by the Assembly to the

following entities: the Leadership Council of the Church of God and its two divisions, Church and Ministry Service and World Service; the Board of Christian Education; the Mass Communications Board; the Missionary Board; Vision-2-Grow; the Departments of Home Missions and Church Growth (from the Board of Church Extension); and curriculum, books, and periodicals (from Warner Press, Inc.).

Commissions
The Commission of Christian Higher Education and the Commission on Social Concerns no longer exist.

Leadership Council
In 1991, the General Assembly renamed the Executive Council as the Leadership Council. (See entry for Church of God Ministries, Inc.)

Gardner College
In 1980, Alberta Bible Institute became Gardner Bible College, and in 1994 Gardner College.

Global Missions
As part of the national agencies reorganization in 1997, the Missionary Board of the Church of God became Global Missions, a department of Church of God Ministries, Inc. (see entry).

Hispanic Council of the Church of God
Today, the Spanish American Council of the Church of God is known as the Hispanic Council of the Church of God (Concilio Hispano de la Iglesia de Dios), or simply the Concilio.

Kima International School of Theology
In 1995, Kima Theological College was reorganized as Kima International School of Theology.

Mid-America Christian University
South Texas Bible Institute became Gulf Coast Bible College, which in 1985 changed its name to Mid-America Bible College and moved from Houston to a new campus in Oklahoma City, Oklahoma. In 2003, the school became Mid-America Christian University.

Vital Christianity
In 1962, the *Gospel Trumpet* was renamed *Vital Christianity*. *Vital Christianity* ceased publication in 1996.

West Indies Theological College
The West Indies Bible Institute is now West Indies Theological College (WITC).

World Ministry Advance
The World Service responsibilities for the World Ministries Budget and functions associated with fund-raising and planned giving are now the responsibility of World Ministry Advance, a department of Church of God Ministries (see entry).

INDEX OF PROPER NAMES

www.ingramcontent.com/pod-product-compliance
Lightning Source LLC
LaVergne TN
LVHW051224240826
846221LV00007B/86